E S T A T E   P U B

FOLKESTONE
DOVER
DEAL

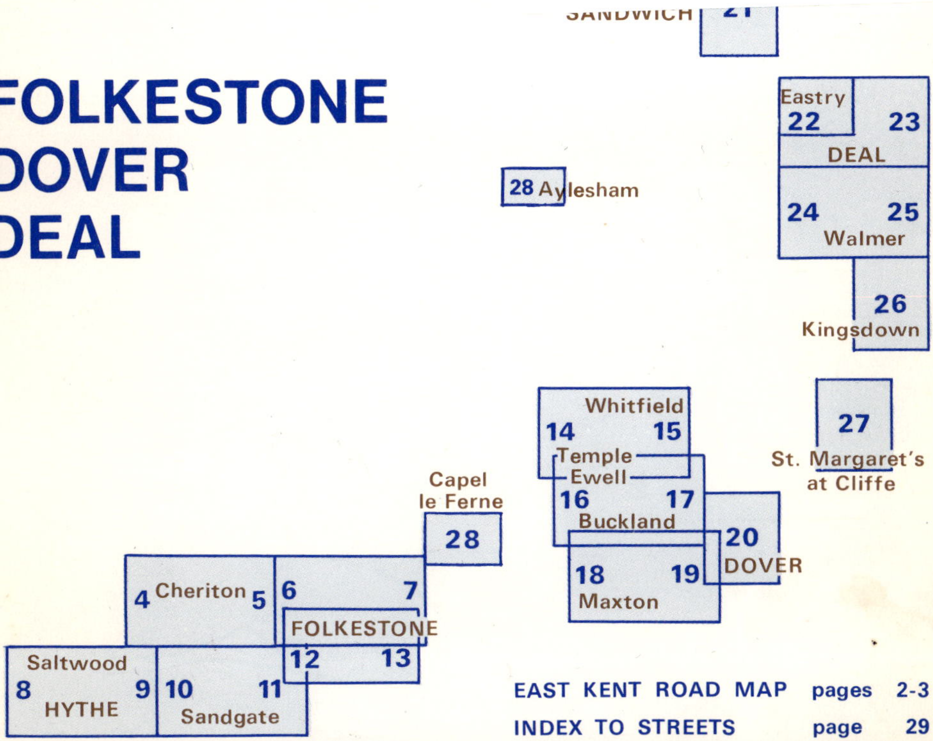

One-way street	→
Car Park	P
Post Office	●
Public Convenience	C
Church	+
Scale of street plans	4 inches to 1 mile

Sreet plans prepared and published by ESTATE PUBLICATIONS, Bridewell House, Tenterden, Kent and based upon the ORDNANCE SURVEY maps with the sanction of the controller of H.M. Stationery Office.

ISBN 0 86084 320 3

ROAD MAP

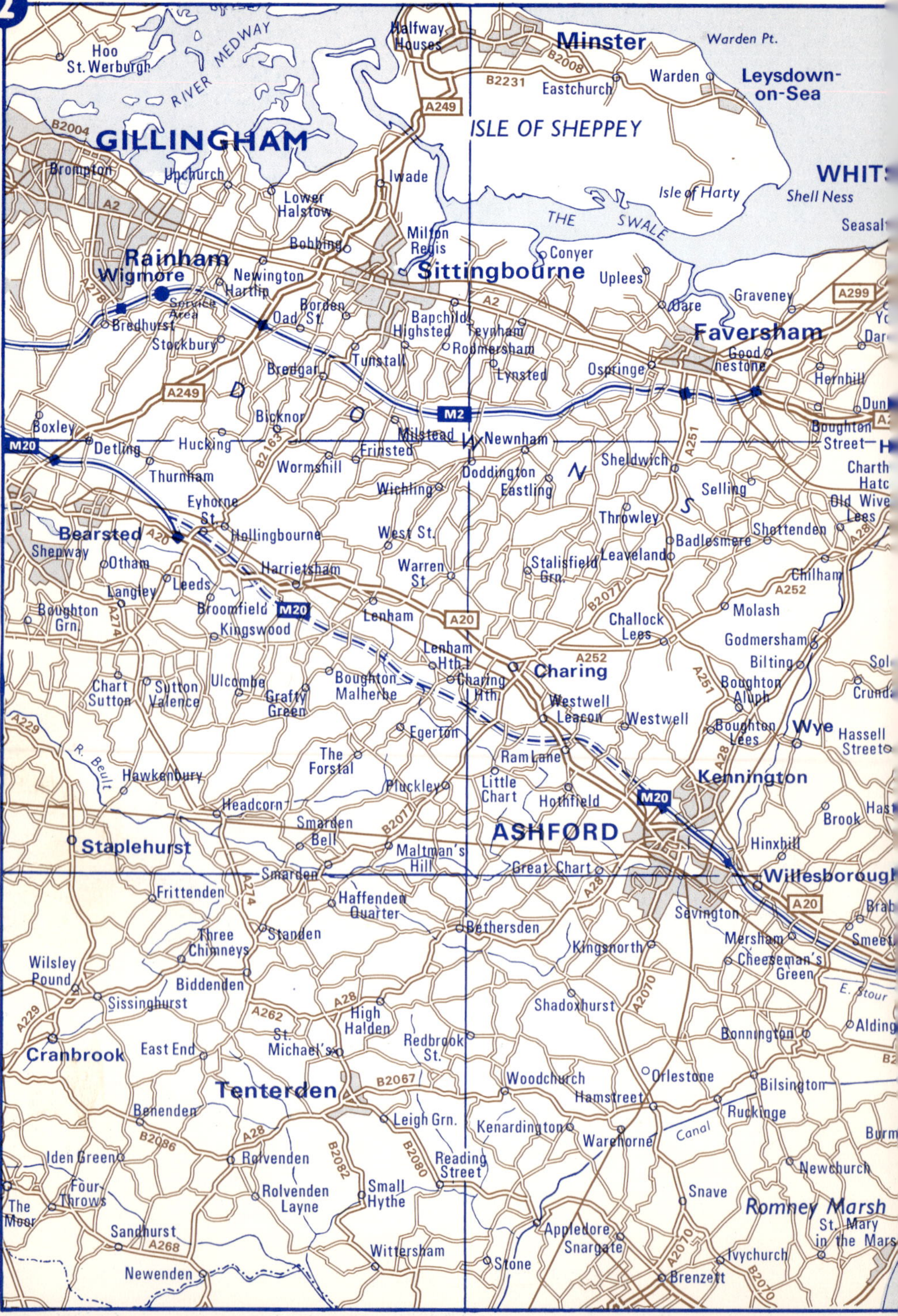
Hoo
St. Werburgh
RIVER MEDWAY
Halfway
Houses
Minster
B2008
Warden Pt.
Warden
Leysdown-
on-Sea
B2231
Eastchurch
A249
ISLE OF SHEPPEY
B2004
GILLINGHAM
Brompton
Upchurch
Lower
Halstow
Iwade
WHITS
Shell Ness
Seasal
Isle of Harty
THE SWALE
A2
Bobbing
Milton
Regis
Rainham
Wigmore
Newington
Hartlip
Sittingbourne
Conyer
Uplees
A278
Service
Area
Bredhurst
Borden
Oad St.
Bapchild
Highsted
Teynham
A2
Oare
Graveney
A299
Faversham
Stockbury
Tunstall
Rodmersham
Lynsted
Ospringe
Good
nestone
Hernhill
Bredgar
A249
D
O
W
N
S
Bicknor
M2
Boxley
Milstead
Newnham
Boughton
Street
M20
Detling
Hucking
B2163
Frinsted
A251
Sheldwich
Thurnham
Wormshill
Doddington
Charth
Hatc
Wichling
Eastling
Selling
Old Wive
Lees
Eyhorne
St.
Throwley
Bearsted
A20
Hollingbourne
West St.
Badlesmere
Shottenden
Shepway
A28
Otham
Harrietsham
Warren
St.
Stalisfield
Grn.
Leaveland
Chilham
A252
Langley
Leeds
B2077
Boughton
Grn.
A274
Broomfield
M20
Lenham
A20
Challock
Lees
Molash
Kingswood
Godmersham
Lenham
Hth.
A252
Bilting
Charing
Chart
Sutton
Sutton
Valence
Ulcombe
Boughton
Malherbe
Charing
Hth.
A251
Boughton
Aluph
Crund
Grafty
Green
Westwell
Leacon
Westwell
A229
Egerton
Boughton
Lees
Wye
Hassell
Street
R. Beult
The
Forstal
Ram Lane
A28
Kennington
Hawkenbury
Pluckley
Little
Chart
Hothfield
M20
Brook
Headcorn
Smarden
Bell
B2077
ASHFORD
Staplehurst
Maltman's
Hill
Hinxhill
Smarden
Great Chart
A28
Willesborough
A274
Frittenden
Haffenden
Quarter
A20
Sevington
Standen
Bethersden
Three
Chimneys
Kingsnorth
Mersham
Smeet
Cheeseman's
Green
Wilsley
Pound
Biddenden
E. Stour
A229
Sissinghurst
A28
High
Halden
A262
Shadoxhurst
A2070
Aldington
St.
Michael's
Redbrook
St.
Bonnington
Cranbrook
East End
Orlestone
Tenterden
B2067
Woodchurch
Bilsington
Hamstreet
Benenden
Leigh Grn.
Ruckinge
B2086
A28
Kenardington
Warehorne
Canal
Iden Green
B2082
B2080
Rolvenden
Reading
Street
Newchurch
The
Moor
Four
Throws
Rolvenden
Layne
Small
Hythe
Snave
Romney Marsh
Sandhurst
A268
Appledore
Snargate
A2070
St. Mary
in the Marsh
Wittersham
Stone
Ivychurch
Newenden
Brenzett
B2070

MARGATE
Cliftonville
Foreness Pt.
Westgate on Sea
Minnis Bay
HERNE BAY
Swalecliffe
Reculver
Hillborough
A299
Birchington
St. Peter's
NORTH FORELAND
Broadstairs
ISLE OF THANET
Acol
St. Nicholas at Wade
Broomfield
Herne
Boyden Gate
Chestfield
Minster
A253
RAMSGATE
Sarre
Chislet
Hoath
Cliffsend
R. Stour
W. Stourmouth
E.
Westmarsh
Pegwell Bay
Broadoak
Hersden
Grove
Tyler Hill
Westbere
Stodmarsh
Sturry
Fordwich
Preston
Elmstone
Hoaden
Great Stonar
Wickhambreux
CANTERBURY
Sandwich
Ash
Littlebourne
Ickham
Wingham
Marshborough
Woodnesborough
Thanington
Bekesbourne
Staple
Worth
Patrixbourne
Goodnestone
Eastry
Ham
Nackington
Bridge
Adisham
Knowlton
Lower Hardres
Chillenden
Sholden
Aylesham
Nonington
Bettes hanger
North bourne
DEAL
Bishopsbourne
Kingston
Tilmanstone
Womenswold
Elvington
Gt. Mongeham
Walmer
Bossingham
Barham
Barfreston
Eythorne
E. Studdal
Ripple
Darringstone
Woolage Green
Sutton
Kingsdown
Stelling Minnis
Shepherdswell
Ringwould
Denton
Coldred
W. Langdon
E. Langdon
Whitfield
Wootton
Lydden
Guston
St. Margaret's at Cliffe
Elmsted Court
Temple Ewell
Ewell Minnis
West Cliffe
Elham
Swingfield Minnis
Buckland
Rhodes Minnis
Alkham
Sth. Foreland
Stowting
Densole
DOVER
Lyminge
Paddlesworth
W. Hougham
Hawkinge
Etchinghill
Capel le Ferne
Postling
Stanford
Newington
A20
Saltwood
FOLKESTONE
Sandgate
Hythe
A259
ymchurch
ary's

NEWINGTON

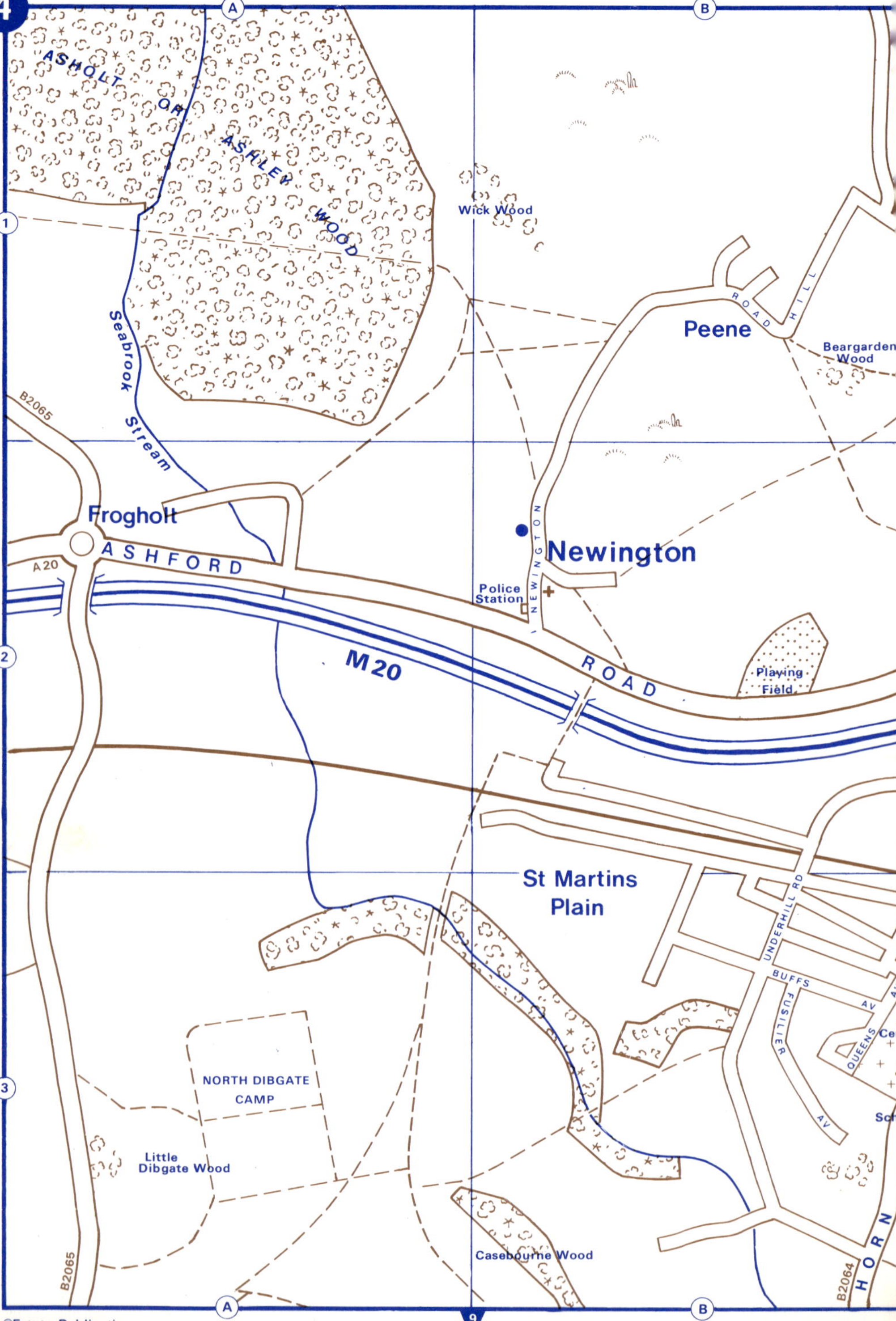
A
B
1
2
3
ASHOLT OR ASHLEY WOOD
Wick Wood
Seabrook Stream
Peene
ROAD
HILL
Beargarden Wood
B2065
Frogholt
ASHFORD
A20
NEWINGTON
Newington
Police Station
M20
ROAD
Playing Field
St Martins Plain
UNDERHILL RD
BUFFS
AV
FUSILIER
AV
QUEENS
AV
Cem
Scho
NORTH DIBGATE CAMP
Little Dibgate Wood
Casebourne Wood
B2065
B2064
HORN

9

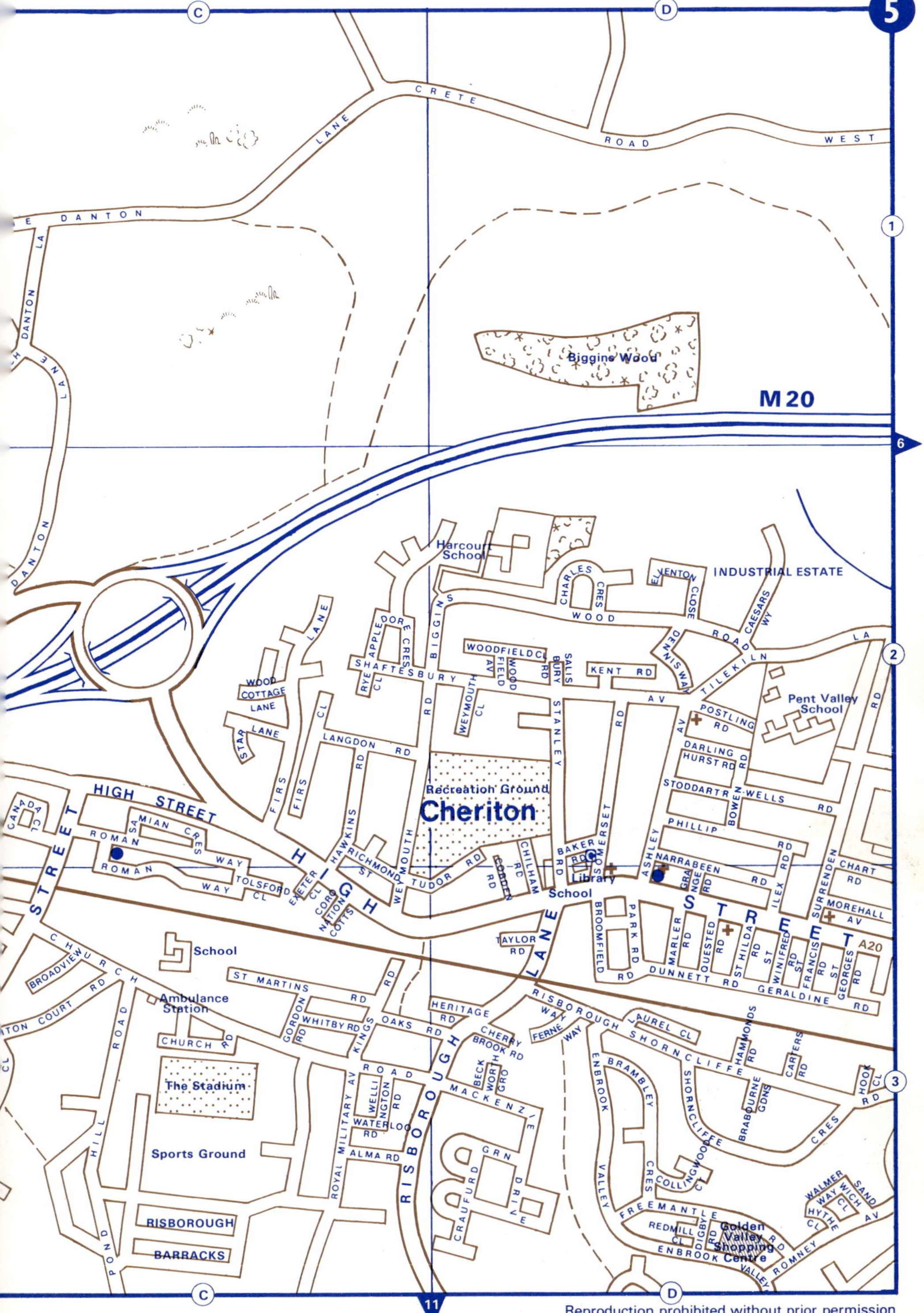
C
D
CRETE
ROAD
WEST
LANE
DANTON
DANTON
LANE
1
Biggins Wood
M20
6
Harcourt School
INDUSTRIAL ESTATE
ELVENTON
CLOSE
CAESARS WY
CHARLES CRES
WOOD
ROAD
DENNIS WAY
TILEKILN LA
2
WOODFIELD CL
WOODFIELD AV
SALISBURY RD
KENT RD
AV
BIGGINS
APPLEDORE CRES
RYE CL
SHAFTESBURY
WEYMOUTH CL
STANLEY
POSTLING RD
Pent Valley School
RD
WOOD COTTAGE LANE
STAR LANE
LANGDON RD
FIRS CL
FIRS
DARLING HURST RD
STODDART RD
WELLS
BOWEN
PHILLIP
HIGH STREET
Recreation Ground
Cheriton
CANADA CL
SAMIAN CRES
ROMAN WAY
TOLSFORD CL
HAWKINS
RICHMOND ST
WEYMOUTH
TUDOR RD
CHILHAM RD
CORNWALLIS RD
BAKER RD
SOMERSET RD
ASHLEY AV
NARRABEEN RD
GRANGE RD
ILEX RD
SURRENDEN
CHART RD
MOREHALL AV
Library
School
STREET
HIGH
EXETER CL
CORONATION COTTS
BROOMFIELD
PARK RD
MARLER RD
QUESTED RD
ST HILDA RD
ST WINIFRED RD
ST FRANCIS RD
ST GEORGES RD
A20
TAYLOR RD
LANE
DUNNETT RD
GERALDINE RD
CHURCH
BROADVIEW
School
ST MARTINS RD
Ambulance Station
COURT RD
CHURCH RD
GORDON RD
WHITBY RD
KINGS OAKS RD
HERITAGE RD
RISBOROUGH WAY
FERNE WAY
LAUREL CL
SHORNCLIFFE RD
HAMMONDS RD
CARTERS RD
HOOK CL
3
CHERRY BROOK RD
BECKWORTH GRO
ROAD
The Stadium
WELLINGTON RD
WATERLOO RD
ALMA RD
ROYAL MILITARY AV
MACKENZIE DRIVE
GRN
CRAUFURD
RISBOROUGH
ENBROOK VALLEY
BRAMBLEY CRES
SHORNCLIFFE CRES
BRABOURNE GDNS
COLLINGWOOD CT
FREEMANTLE RD
REDMILL CL
DIGBY RD
Golden Valley Shopping Centre
ENBROOK VALLEY
Sports Ground
HILL ROAD
POND
RISBOROUGH BARRACKS
WALMER WAY
SANDWICH CL
HYTHE CL
ROMNEY AV
11
C
D

FOLKESTONE

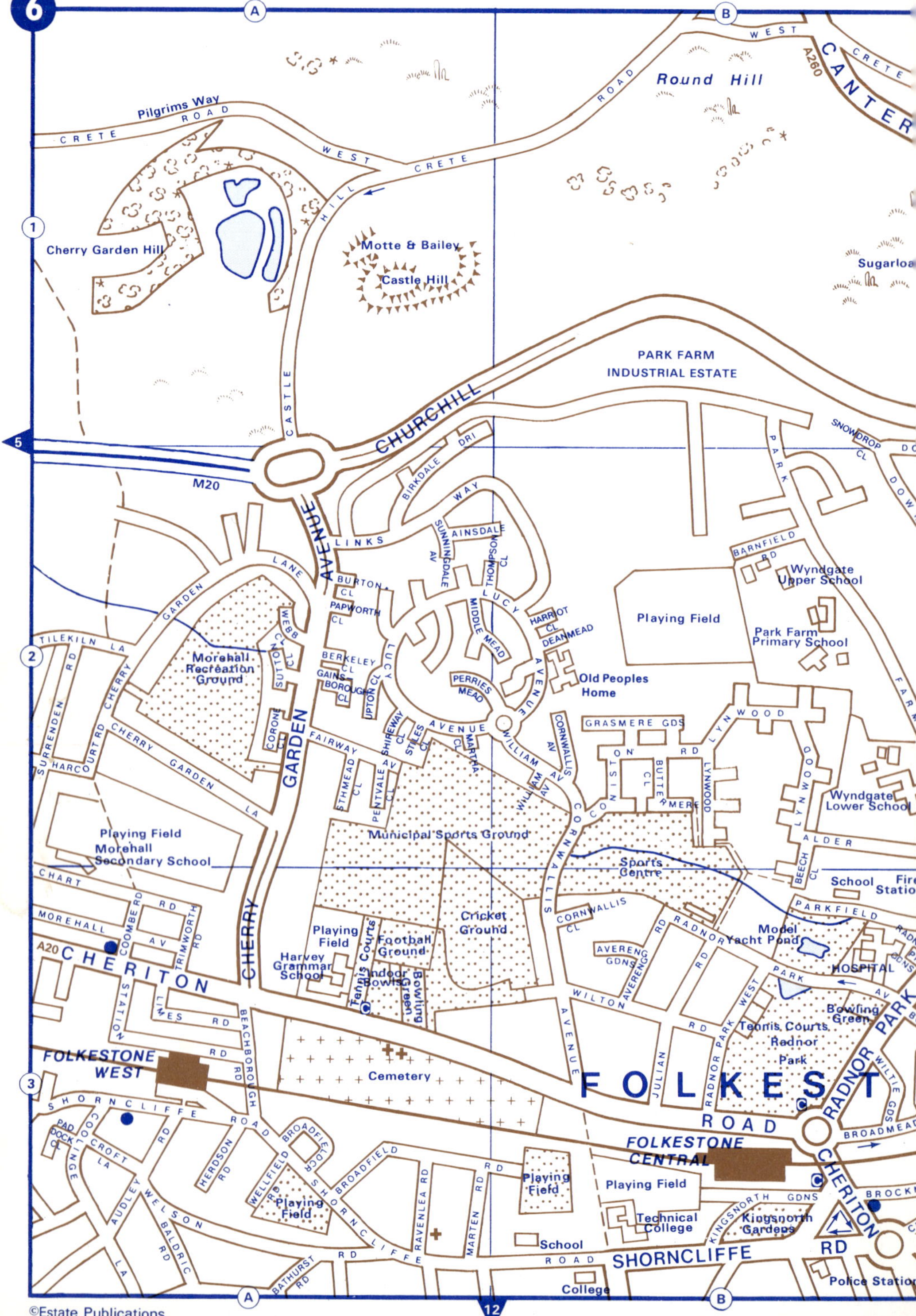
A
B
1
2
3
5
12
Pilgrims Way
CRETE ROAD
WEST
CRETE
ROAD
WEST CRETE
A260
CANTER
Round Hill
Cherry Garden Hill
HILL
CASTLE
Motte & Bailey
Castle Hill
Sugarloa
PARK FARM
INDUSTRIAL ESTATE
CHURCHILL
M20
SNOWDROP CL
BIRKDALE DRI
WAY
AVENUE
LINKS
AINSDALE
SUNNINGDALE AV
THOMPSON CL
LANE
GARDEN
BURTON CL
PAPWORTH CL
LUCY
MIDDLE MEAD
HARRIOT CL
DEANMEAD
BARNFIELD RD
Wyndgate Upper School
Playing Field
Park Farm Primary School
TILEKILN LA
RD
Morehall Recreation Ground
WEBB CL
SUTTON CL
BERKELEY CL
GAINSBOROUGH CL
UPTON CL
PERRIES MEAD
Old Peoples Home
FARM
CHERRY
SURRENDEN
HARCOURT RD
CHERRY GARDEN LA
CORONE CL
FAIRWAY
SHIREWAY CL
STILES CL
MARTHA CL
WILLIAM AV
CORNWALLIS AV
GRASMERE GDS
LYNWOOD
CONISTON RD
BUTTERMERE CL
STHMEAD CL
PENTVALE AV
Wyndgate Lower School
Playing Field
Morehall Secondary School
Municipal Sports Ground
CORNWALLIS
Sports Centre
ALDER
BEECH CL
School
Fire Station
CHART
COOMBE RD
RD
TRIMWORTH RD
MOREHALL AV
A20 CHERITON
Playing Field
Football Ground
Harvey Grammar School
Tennis Courts
Indoor Bowls
Bowling Green
Cricket Ground
CORNWALLIS CL
RADNOR
Model Yacht Pond
PARKFIELD
AVERENG GDNS
AVERENG RD
HOSPITAL
PARK
WILTON
WEST
STATION
LIMES RD
BEACHBOROUGH RD
Bowling Green
Tennis Courts
Radnor Park
FOLKESTONE WEST
Cemetery
AVENUE
JULIAN RD
RADNOR PARK RD
FOLKEST
RADNOR PARK
WILTIE GDS
BROADMEAD
SHORNCLIFFE ROAD
PADDOCK CL
COOLINGE LA
CROFT
HERDSON RD
BROADFIELD
ELDER
WELLFIELD RD
FOLKESTONE CENTRAL
Playing Field
Playing Field
Playing Field
Technical College
Kingsnorth Gardens
KINGSNORTH GDNS
BROCKMA
CHERITON RD
AUDLEY
WELSON
BALDRIC RD
RAVENLEA RD
MARTEN RD
School
SHORNCLIFFE
BATHURST RD
College
Police Station

C
D
1
2
3
13
Pilgrims Way
CRETEWAY DOWN
CRETE ROAD EAST
A20
The Valiant Sailor PH
HILL
Wingate Hill
MONTGOMERY
GEORGE
PLIMSOLL AV
CRETE WAY
GURR CRES
FLEMING
BRABNER CL
WAY
SPRING WELL AV
SUGARLOAF WK
AVENUE
ROAD
HILL RD
DOVER HILL
WALTON MANOR CL
CALGARY CRES
PAGET PL
BEATTY
BEATTY CL
PARK VW
WAY
DALLAS BRETT
KEYES PL
CRES
DOVER RD
STANBURY
CRESCENT
HOLLANDS AV
RD
WOOD
Liby
RITA PL
LA
WINGATE RD
GDNS
JOYES CL
JOYES
IVY
GREEN
INGOLDSBY
TENNYSON PL
BROWNING PL
RD
WEAR BAY RD
BOWLES WELL GDNS
Martello Tower
WALTON
CANTERBURY
ATHELSTAN RD
ETHELBERT RD
INVICTA
ST
GREENFIELD
LA
ST
TYSON
ROAD
School
Playing Field
DOLPHINS
Black Bull P.H.
MARSHALL RD
JAMES ST
GREEN
CANTERBURY
School
ROAD
SIDNEY
BRIDGE
ST
ALEXANDRA
DENMARK
ST
PRINCESS
ST
STUART RD
DOVER
CLO
WARREN
WARREN WAY
WHITECLIFF WAY
BAY
MEAD
RD
School
ERNWELL RD
ALBION RD
CRES
ALBERT RD
WALTON
FERN BK CRES
BLACK BULL RD
RUSSELL RD
GARDEN
JESMOND ST
LINDEN
DAWSON
ARCHER
Recreation Ground
GLADSTONE RD
STATION APP
THANET GDS
FORELAND AV
Bowling Green
Tennis Courts
PAVILION RD
RADNOR PK
SHEPWAY CLO
Youth Centre
BOLTON RD
ROAD
EASTFIELDS
MORRISON RD
FOLLY RD
WARREN RD
CRES
RD
Martello Tower
PALMERSTON
STONE
BRAD AV
FOORD
SUSSEX ROAD
BRADSTONE AV
DEVON RD
ROAD
ABBOTT RD
GROVE
ROSS GDS
RENDALE RD
ORMONDE RD
ENDALE
MARTELLO RD
BURROW RD
PENFOLD
SEAGRAVE CR
HASBOROUGH RD
VARNE RD
Miniature Golf Links
East Cliff Pavilion
SOUTH BOURNE RD
SEAGRAVE RD
PETER ST
QUEEN ST
LENNARD RD
DUDLEY RD
EAST CLIFF
WEAR BAY
PL
BAY
WEAR
RD
E
BRADSTONE NEW RD
BRADSTONE
MNT PLEASANT
ST JOHNS
CLARENCE
BELLEVUE
Schools
DOVER ST
HARVEY
CHARLOTTE ST
RYLAND
RADNOR BRIDGE RD
HARBOUR WAY
LONDON ST
ELM STEAD PL
TRAM
DYKE
E CLIFF GDS
East Cliff
WEAR BAY RD
East Cliff Triangle
PARADE
CORONATION
DARBY RD
GUILDHALL
DARLINGTON ST
DARBY PL
CAMBRIDGE GDS
CONNAUGHT RD
TONTINE
ST MICHAELS ST
RD
GRACE HILL
DOVER RD
Sch Liby
MILL BAY
NORTH ST
THE DURLOCKS
School
EAST ST
STADE
THE
VICTORIA GR
COPTHALL GDS
FORESTERS WAY
SHELLONS ST
ROAD
THE
Town Hall
GUILDHALL ST
RENDEZVOUS ST
HIGH ST
MILL FLD
East Pier

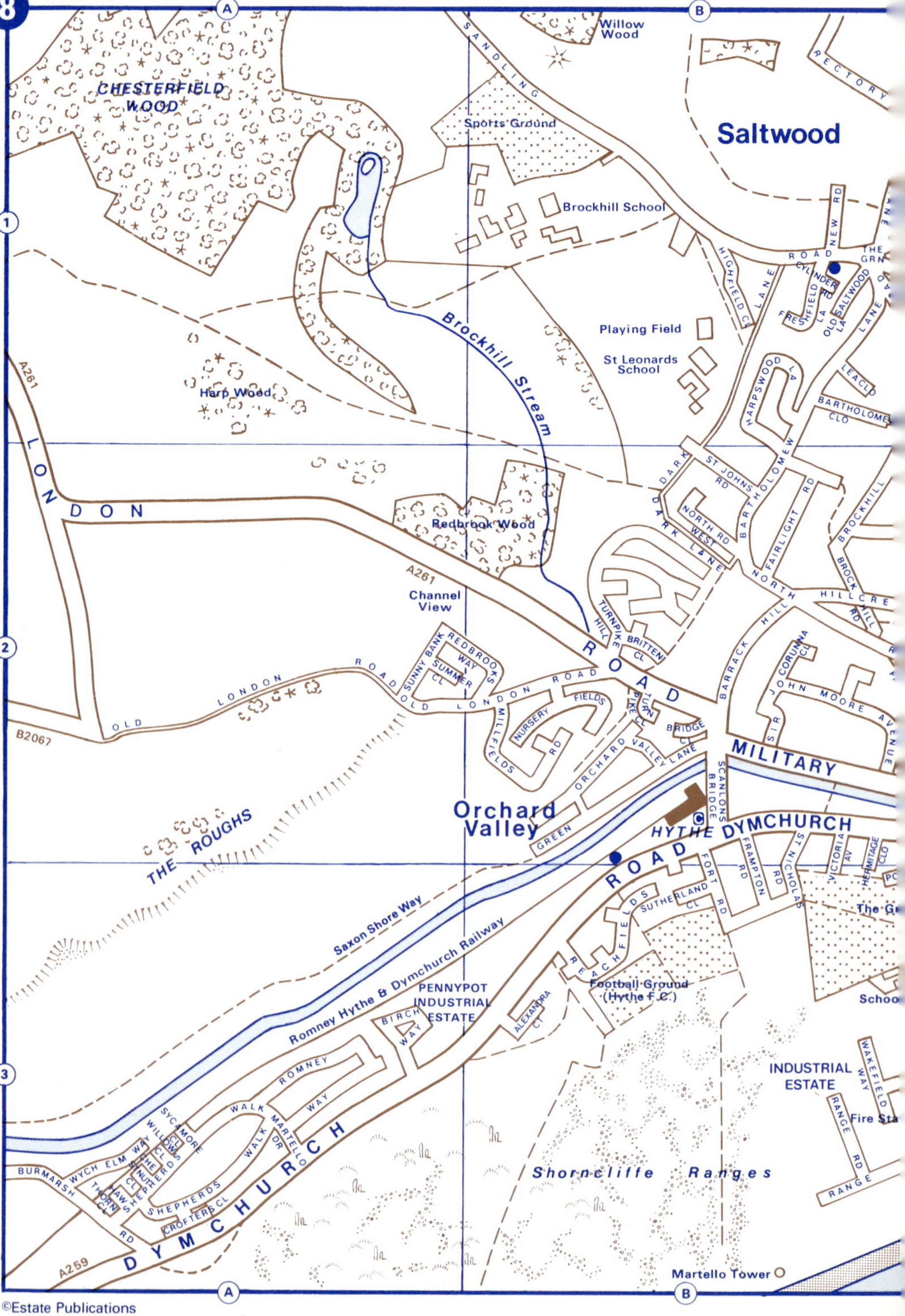
A
B
1
2
3
Willow Wood
SANDLING
RECTORY
CHESTERFIELD WOOD
Sports Ground
Saltwood
Brockhill School
NEW RD
THE GRN
ROAD
CYLINDER RD
HIGHFIELD CL
LANE
FRESHFIELD LA
OLD SALTWOOD LA
LANE
Brockhill Stream
Playing Field
St Leonards School
HARPSWOOD LA
LEACLD
BARTHOLOMEW CLO
A261
Harp Wood
LONDON
ST JOHNS RD
DARK LANE
BARTHOLOMEW
FAIRLIGHT RD
BROCKHILL
Redbrook Wood
NORTH RD WEST
NORTH
BROCK HILL RD
HILLCREST RD
Channel View
TURNPIKE HILL
BRITTEN CL
ROAD
BARRACK HILL
CORUNNA CL
JOHN MOORE AVENUE
SIR
REDBROOKS WAY
SUNNY BANK
SUMMER CL
OLD LONDON ROAD
MILLFIELDS
NURSERY RD
FIELDS
TURNPIKE CL
BRIDGE CL
ORCHARD VALLEY LANE
SCANLONS BRIDGE
MILITARY
B2067
Orchard Valley
GREEN
THE ROUGHS
HYTHE DYMCHURCH ROAD
FRAMPTON RD
ST NICHOLAS RD
VICTORIA AV
HERMITAGE CLO
FORT RD
SUTHERLAND CL
REACHFIELDS
The G
Saxon Shore Way
Romney Hythe & Dymchurch Railway
PENNYPOT INDUSTRIAL ESTATE
BIRCH WAY
ALEXANDRA CT
Football Ground (Hythe F.C.)
Schoo
INDUSTRIAL ESTATE
WAKEFIELD WAY
RANGE RD
RANGE
Fire Sta
ROMNEY WAY
WALK
MARTELLO DR
SYCAMORE CL
WILLOWS
WYCH ELM WAY
THE CHESTNUTS
BURMARSH RD
HAWTHORN CT
SHEPHERDS
SHEPHERDS WALK
CROFTERS CL
DYMCHURCH
Shorncliffe Ranges
A259
Martello Tower

C
D
1
2
3
10
Orchard Field Shaw
Blackhouse Shaw
Ash Plantation
Saltwood Castle
B2065
HILL
School
THE CLOSE
CASTLE
CASTLE CRES
Cricket Ground
ROAD
TANNERS
TANNERS HILL
Mill Leese Shaw
Golf Club House
BASSET CLO
BASSET GDNS
BLACKHOUSE RISE
FARMER CLO
CLIFF CLO
CLIFF
PARK
SENE PARK
SENE
Golf Course
LOOKERS LA
AVENUE
CASTLE AV
QUARRY CL
LANE
GDNS
DEEDES CL
NEWINGTON MEADOW
BLACKHOUSE
CANNONGATE
RD
MILL LA
LOWER BLACKHOUSE HILL
CANNONGATE AV
CANNONGATE GDNS
ROAD
STATION ROAD
TANNERS HILL
FOYSP
HAFOD PASS
NORTH
CHURCH
OAK WK
CHURCH
THE DENE
STREET
MILL RD
INN
BELL
ALBION PL
ELM GDS
CANNONGATE CL
Playing Field
A259
STREET
EAST ST
SEABROOK ROAD
SIDE
MALTHOUSE HILL
OAK
Sch
MKT HILL
DENTAL
KINGS HD YA
DOUGLAS AV
WILLIAM PITT CL
TWISS GRO
TWISS
EARLSFIELD
THOLOMEW
Town Hall
HIGH
MALTHOUSE HILL
BANK ST
MOUNT ST
MARINE WK ST
PROSPECT
COBBS PAS
THEATRE RD
SUN LA
Police Station
Clinic
TWISS AV
Royal Military Canal
Red Lion Hotel
CHAPEL ST
RAMPART
NEW PROSPECT
THE
AVENUE
COBAY CL
STURDY CLO
Golf Links
LAND
RD
PORTLAND RD
Bowling Club
Municipal Offices
Liby
STADE
LADIES
Hythe Tennis Club
LUCYS
Cricket Ground
WALK
Schools
WOOD RD
FISHER CLO
ROAD
Hotel Imperial
PARADE
WINDMILL ST
NAPIER GDNS
WAKEFIELD
Recreation Ground
ALBERT
ELIZABETH GDS
LYNTON RD
ALBERT LA
TOWER GDNS
WALK
Recreation Ground
Tennis Courts
Marine Gardens
ROAD
BEACONSFIELD TER
PRINCES
LEONARDS
NEW RD
RD
THE FAIRWAY
SOUTH RD
MOYLE TOWER
PARADE
Pedestrian Walk
PARK
COBDEN RD
VICTORIA RD
ORMONDE RD
STREET
ARTHUR RD
Sailing Club
Cinque Ports Pavilion
MARINE
ROAD
THERESA RD
PARADE
ST HILDAS RD
The Martello Tower
WEST
HYTHE

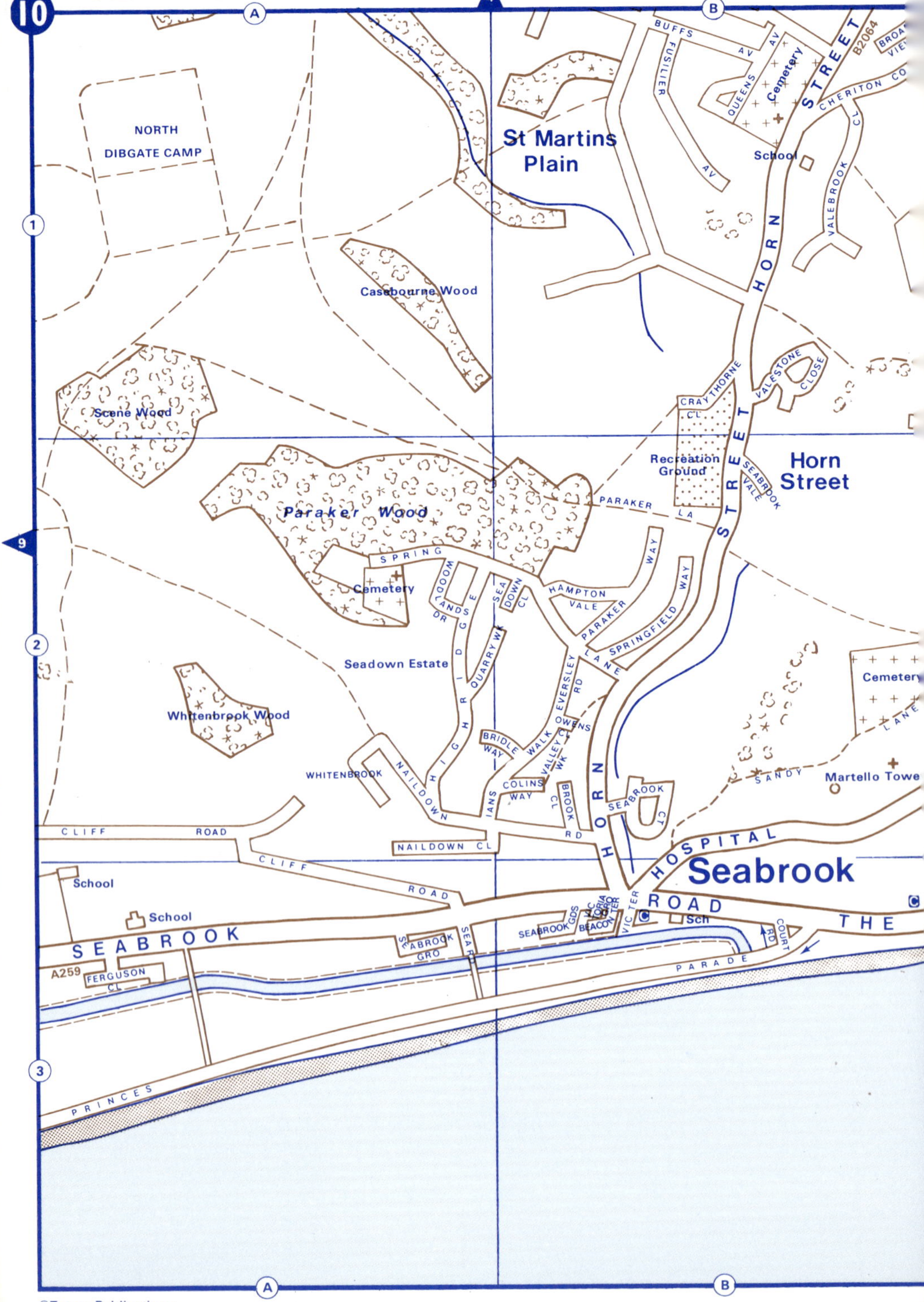

A
B
4
1
2
3
9
NORTH DIBGATE CAMP
St Martins Plain
BUFFS AV
FUSILIER AV
QUEENS
Cemetery
School
B2064
HORN STREET
CHERITON CL
VALEBROOK
Casebourne Wood
Scene Wood
CRAYTHORNE CL
VALESTONE CLOSE
Recreation Ground
Horn Street
SEABROOK VALE
PARAKER LA
Paraker Wood
SPRING
WOODLANDS DR
SEA DOWN CL
HAMPTON VALE
PARAKER WAY
SPRINGFIELD WAY
PARAKER LANE
Cemetery
Seadown Estate
HIGH RIDGE
QUARRY WK
EVERSLEY RD
OWENS
BRIDLE WAY
WALK
VALLEY CL
WK
Whitenbrook Wood
WHITENBROOK
NAILDOWN
COLINS WAY
IANS
BROOK CL
SEABROOK CT
SANDY LANE
Martello Towe
CLIFF ROAD
NAILDOWN CL
RD
HOSPITAL
Seabrook
School
School
ROAD
SEABROOK GDS
VICTORIA GRO
BEACON TER
VIC TER
Sch
COURT RD
THE
SEABROOK
SEABROOK GRO
SEA RD
A259
FERGUSON CL
PARADE
PRINCES

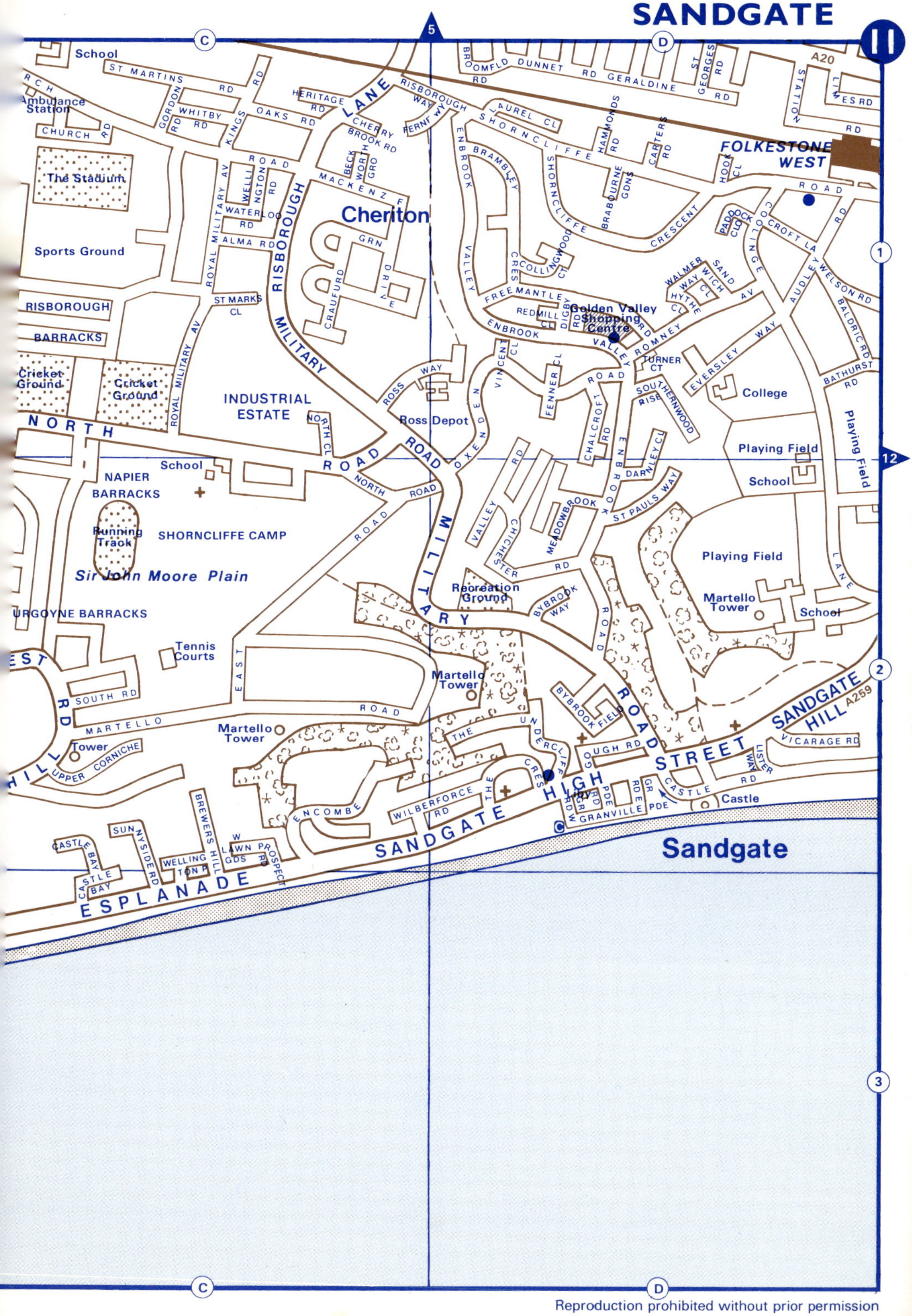
C
5
D
A20
School
ST MARTINS RD
RD
Ambulance Station
CHURCH RD
GORDON RD
WHITBY RD
OAKS RD
KINGS ROAD
HERITAGE RD
LANE
CHERRY BROOK RD
RISBOROUGH WAY
FERNE WY
BROOMFLD RD
DUNNET RD
GERALDINE RD
ST GEORGES RD
STATION RD
LIMES RD
LAUREL CL
SHORNCLIFFE RD
HAMMONDS RD
CARTERS RD
FOLKESTONE WEST
HOOK CL
ROAD
The Stadium
ROYAL MILITARY AV
WELLINGTON RD
WATERLOO RD
ALMA RD
BECKWORTH GRO
MACKENZIE
Cheriton
GRN
DRIVE
CRAUFURD
ENBROOK VALLEY
BRAMBLEY CRES
SHORNCLIFFE CRESCENT
BRABOURNE GDNS
PADDOCK CL
COOLINGE
CROFT LA
RD
Sports Ground
RISBOROUGH
MILITARY ROAD
ST MARKS CL
COLLINGWOOD CT
WALMER WAY
SANDWICH CL
HYTHE CL
AV
AUDLEY
WELSON RD
BALDRIC RD
1
RISBOROUGH
BARRACKS
FREEMANTLE
REDMILL CL
DIGBY RD
Golden Valley Shopping Centre
ENBROOK
VALLEY RD
ROMNEY
WAY
EVERSLEY
Cricket Ground
Cricket Ground
ROSS WAY
VINCENT CL
FENNER CL
ROAD
TURNER CT
SOUTHERNWOOD RISE
College
BATHURST RD
INDUSTRIAL ESTATE
NORTH CL
Ross Depot
OXENDEN
CHALCROFT RD
ENBROOK
DARNLEY CL
Playing Field
Playing Field
NORTH ROAD
ROAD
12
School
NAPIER BARRACKS
NORTH ROAD
ROAD
MILITARY
VALLEY RD
CHICHESTER RD
MEADOWBROOK
ST PAULS WAY
School
Running Track
SHORNCLIFFE CAMP
Playing Field
LANE
Sir John Moore Plain
Recreation Ground
BYBROOK WAY
ROAD
Martello Tower
School
URGOYNE BARRACKS
Tennis Courts
EAST
Martello Tower
BYBROOK FIELD
ROAD
2
SANDGATE HILL
A259
SOUTH RD
RD
ROAD
MARTELLO
Martello Tower
THE UNDERCLIFF
Tower
UPPER CORNICHE
HILL
GOUGH RD
STREET
VICARAGE RD
LISTER WAY
HIGH
CRES
THE
WILBERFORCE RD
ENCOMBE
Liby
RD
PDE
RD E
GR
CASTLE RD
Castle
PDE
GRANVILLE
ROW
SANDGATE
BREWERS HILL
SUNNYSIDE RD
LAWN RD
PROSPECT
W
CASTLE BAY
CASTLE BAY
WELLINGTON P
GDS
ESPLANADE
SANDGATE
Sandgate
3
C
D

FOLKESTONE

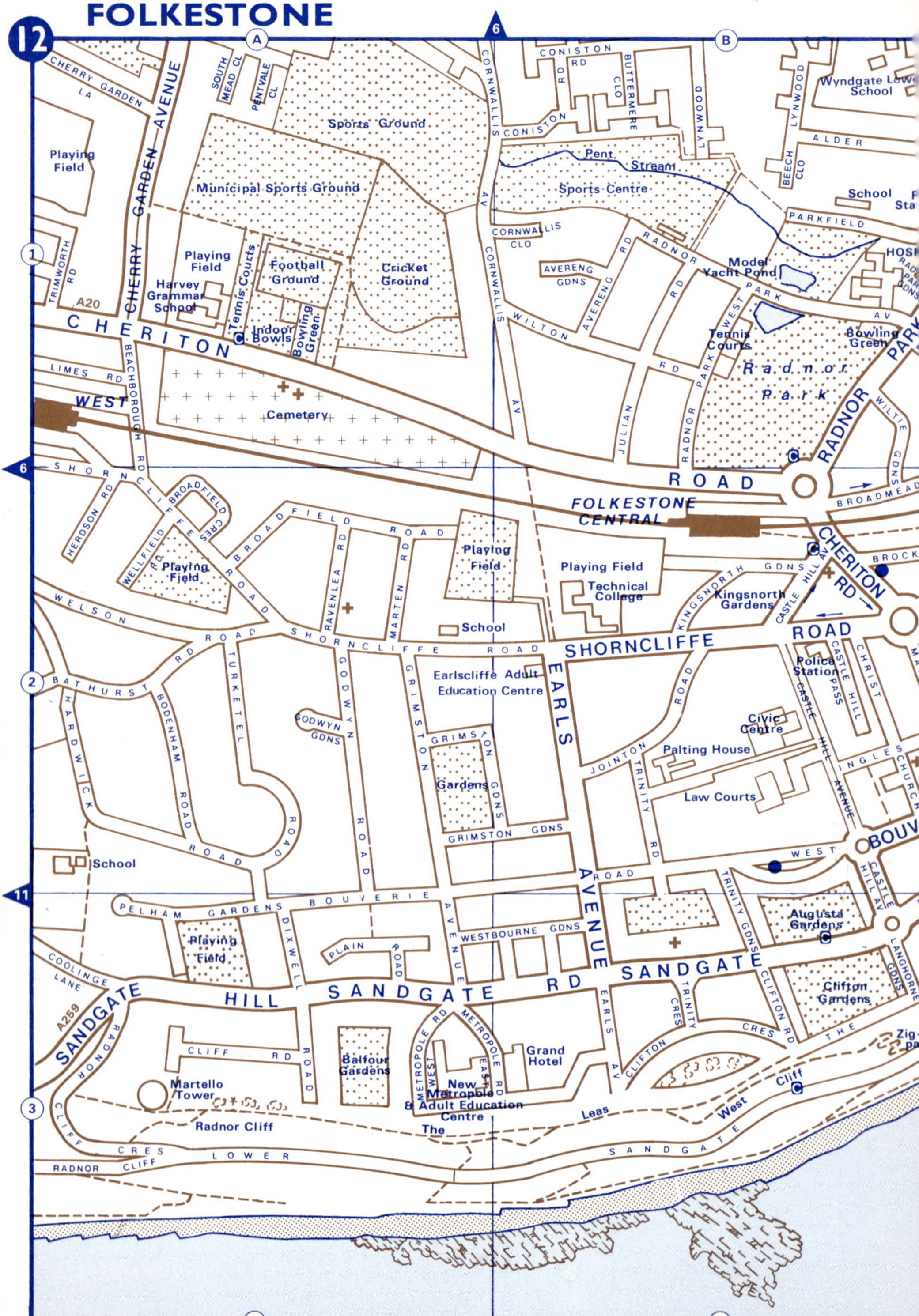
A
B
6
1
2
3
11
CHERRY GARDEN LA
CHERRY GARDEN AVENUE
SOUTH MEAD CL
PENTVALE CL
Playing Field
Sports Ground
Municipal Sports Ground
Playing Field
Harvey Grammar School
Tennis Courts
Football Ground
Cricket Ground
Indoor Bowls
Bowling Green
TRIMWORTH RD
A20
CHERITON
LIMES RD
BEACHBOROUGH RD
WEST
Cemetery
CONISTON RD
CONISTON
BUTTERMERE CLO
LYNWOOD
CORNWALLIS AV
Pent Stream
Sports Centre
CORNWALLIS CLO
AVERENG GDNS
AVERENG RD
RADNOR PARK
WILTON RD
JULIAN AV
RADNOR PARK WEST
RADNOR PARK RD
Model Yacht Pond
Tennis Courts
Radnor Park
Bowling Green
Wyndgate Lower School
LYNWOOD
ALDER
BEECH CLO
School
PARKFIELD
AV
RADNOR PARK
WILTIE GDNS
ROAD
BROADMEAD
SHORNCLIFFE RD
HERDSON RD
BROADFIELD CRES
WELLFIELD RD
Playing Field
BROADFIELD ROAD
RAVENLEA RD
MARTEN RD
Playing Field
FOLKESTONE CENTRAL
Playing Field
Technical College
KINGSNORTH GDNS
Kingsnorth Gardens
CASTLE HILL AV
CHERITON RD
BROCK
WELSON ROAD
School
SHORNCLIFFE ROAD
SHORNCLIFFE
ROAD
BATHURST RD
HARDWICK
TURKETEL
BODENHAM ROAD
GODWYN GDNS
GODWYN ROAD
GRIMSTON AV
Earlscliffe Adult Education Centre
EARLS AVENUE
GRIMSTON GDNS
Gardens
GRIMSTON GDNS
ROAD
JOINTON RD
TRINITY RD
Palting House
Civic Centre
Police Station
CASTLE HILL PASS
CASTLE HILL AVENUE
CHRIST
Law Courts
INGLES
CHURCH
BOUVE
WEST
CASTLE HILL AV
School
PELHAM GARDENS
BOUVERIE
Playing Field
DIXWELL
PLAIN ROAD
WESTBOURNE GDNS
ROAD
TRINITY GDNS
Augusta Gardens
Clifton Gardens
CLIFTON RD
LANGHORNE GDNS
COOLINGE LANE
SANDGATE HILL
SANDGATE RD
SANDGATE
A259
RADNOR
CLIFF RD
ROAD
Balfour Gardens
METROPOLE RD
METROPOLE RD WEST
METROPOLE RD EAST
Grand Hotel
EARLS AV
TRINITY CRES
CRES
CLIFTON
THE
Zig-z path
Martello Tower
Radnor Cliff
New Metropole & Adult Education Centre
The
Leas
West
Cliff
CLIFF CRES
RADNOR CLIFF
LOWER SANDGATE

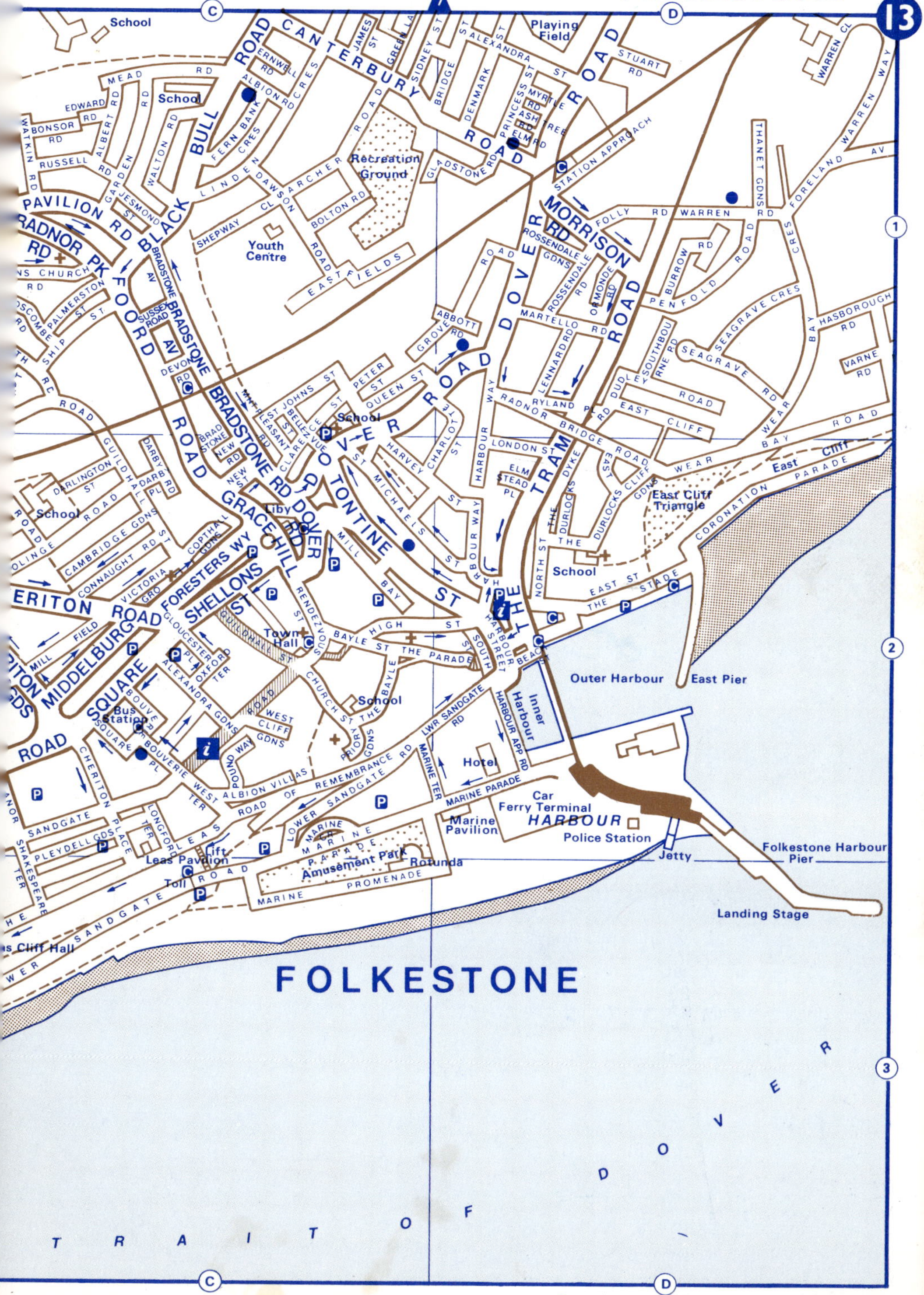
FOLKESTONE
School
Playing Field
CANTERBURY ROAD
ALEXANDRA ST
STUART RD
WARREN CL
WARREN WAY
FORELAND AV
School
Recreation Ground
Youth Centre
Outer Harbour
East Pier
Inner Harbour
HARBOUR
Car Ferry Terminal
Police Station
Marine Pavilion
Hotel
Jetty
Folkestone Harbour Pier
Landing Stage
Amusement Park
Rotunda
Leas Pavilion
Lift
Toll
Town Hall
Bus Station
Liby
East Cliff Triangle
East Cliff
School
MARINE PARADE
MARINE PROMENADE
SANDGATE ROAD
TONTINE ST
DOVER ROAD
FOORD ROAD
GRACE HILL
SHELLONS ST
MIDDELBURG SQUARE
THE TRAM ROAD
MORRISON RD
WEAR BAY ROAD
CORONATION PARADE
THE STADE
STRAIT OF DOVER

TEMPLE EWELL

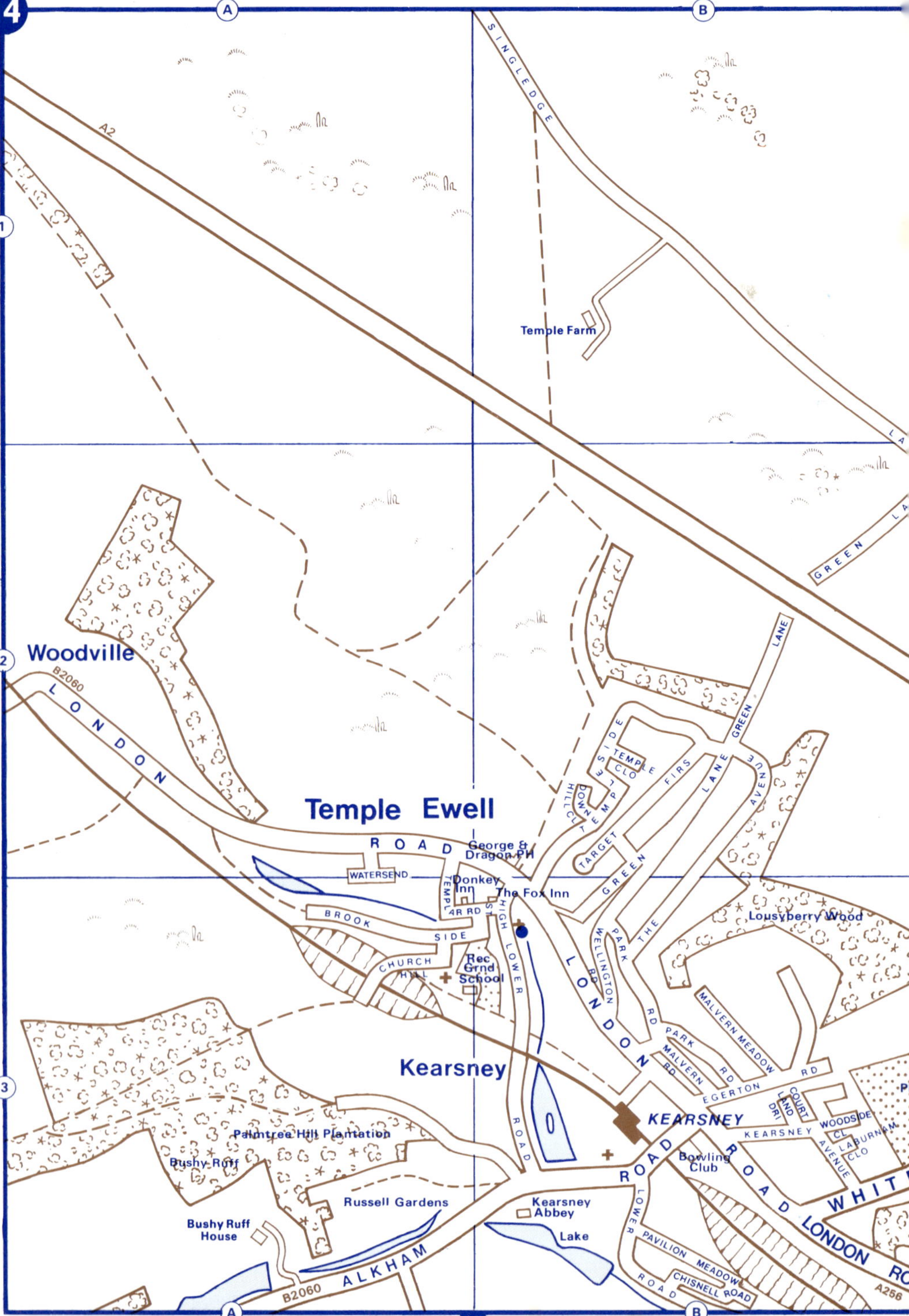

16

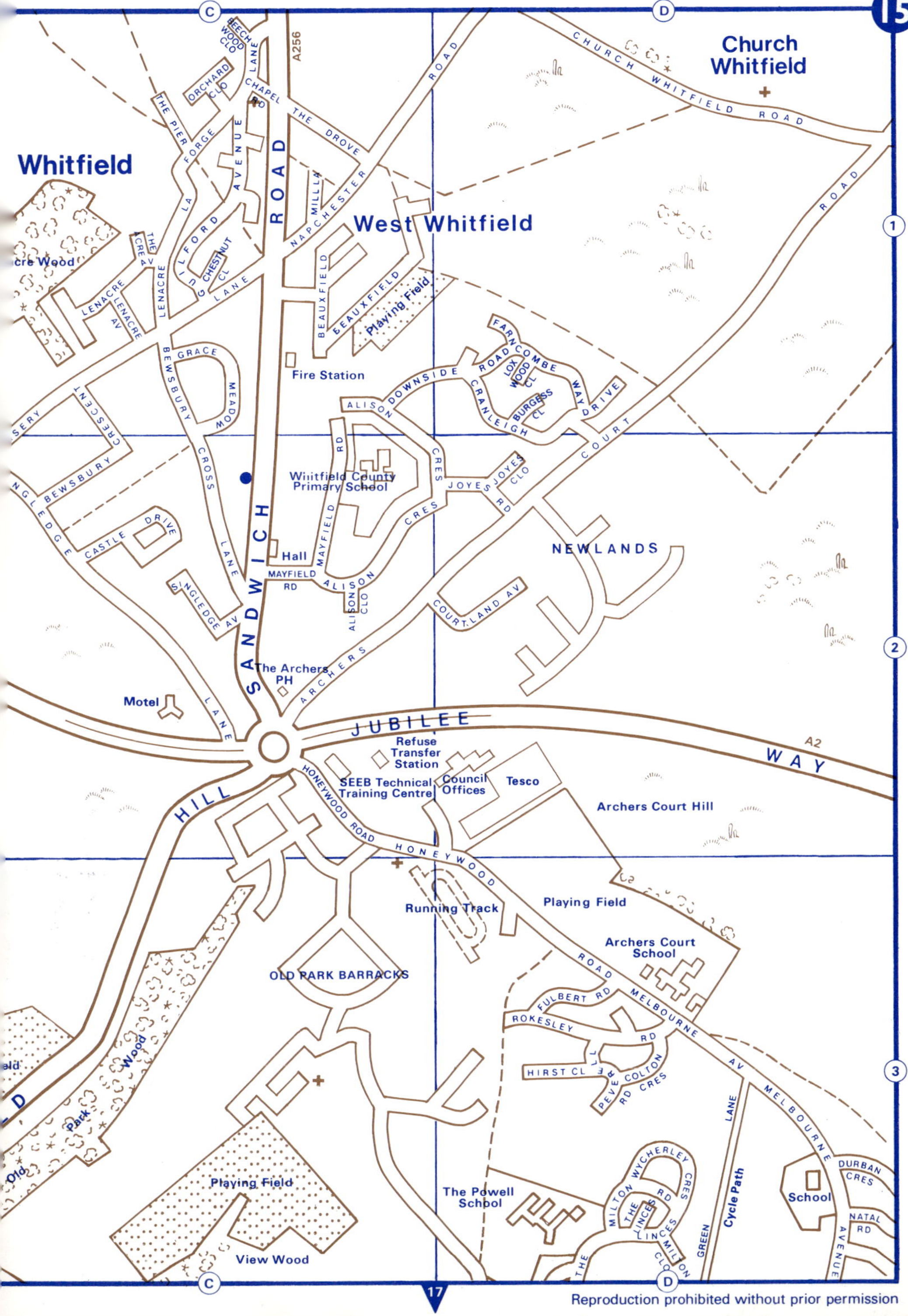
C
D
Church Whitfield
CHURCH WHITFIELD ROAD
ROAD
Whitfield
West Whitfield
A256
SANDWICH ROAD
BEECH WOOD CLO
LANE
ORCHARD CLO
CHAPEL RD
THE DROVE
THE PIER
FORGE LA
AVENUE
NAPCHESTER
MILLLA
ILFORD
THE ACRE AV
CHESTNUT CL
LENACRE
LENACRE AV
LANE
BEAUXFIELD
BEAUXFIELD
Playing Field
Fire Station
GRACE
BEWSBURY
MEADOW
BEWSBURY CRESCENT
CROSS
FARNCOMBE WAY
LOX WOOD CL
ROAD
DOWNSIDE
CRANLEIGH
BURGESS CL
DRIVE
ALISON
COURT
Whitfield County Primary School
RD
CRES
JOYES
JOYES CLO
RD
CRES
CASTLE
DRIVE
SINGLEDGE
SINGLEDGE AV
LANE
Hall
MAYFIELD
MAYFIELD RD
ALISON
ALISON CLO
NEWLANDS
COURTLAND AV
ARCHERS
The Archers PH
Motel
LANE
JUBILEE WAY
A2
Refuse Transfer Station
SEEB Technical Training Centre
Council Offices
Tesco
Archers Court Hill
HILL
HONEYWOOD ROAD
HONEYWOOD
Running Track
Playing Field
Archers Court School
OLD PARK BARRACKS
ROAD
MELBOURNE
FULBERT RD
ROKESLEY
RD
HIRST CL
PEVERELL
COLTON CRES
RD
AV
MELBOURNE
LANE
Cycle Path
GREEN
DURBAN CRES
School
NATAL RD
AVENUE
WYCHERLEY CRES
MILTON RD
THE LINCES
LINCES
MILTON CLO
THE
The Powell School
Playing Field
View Wood
Old Park Wood
1
2
3

17

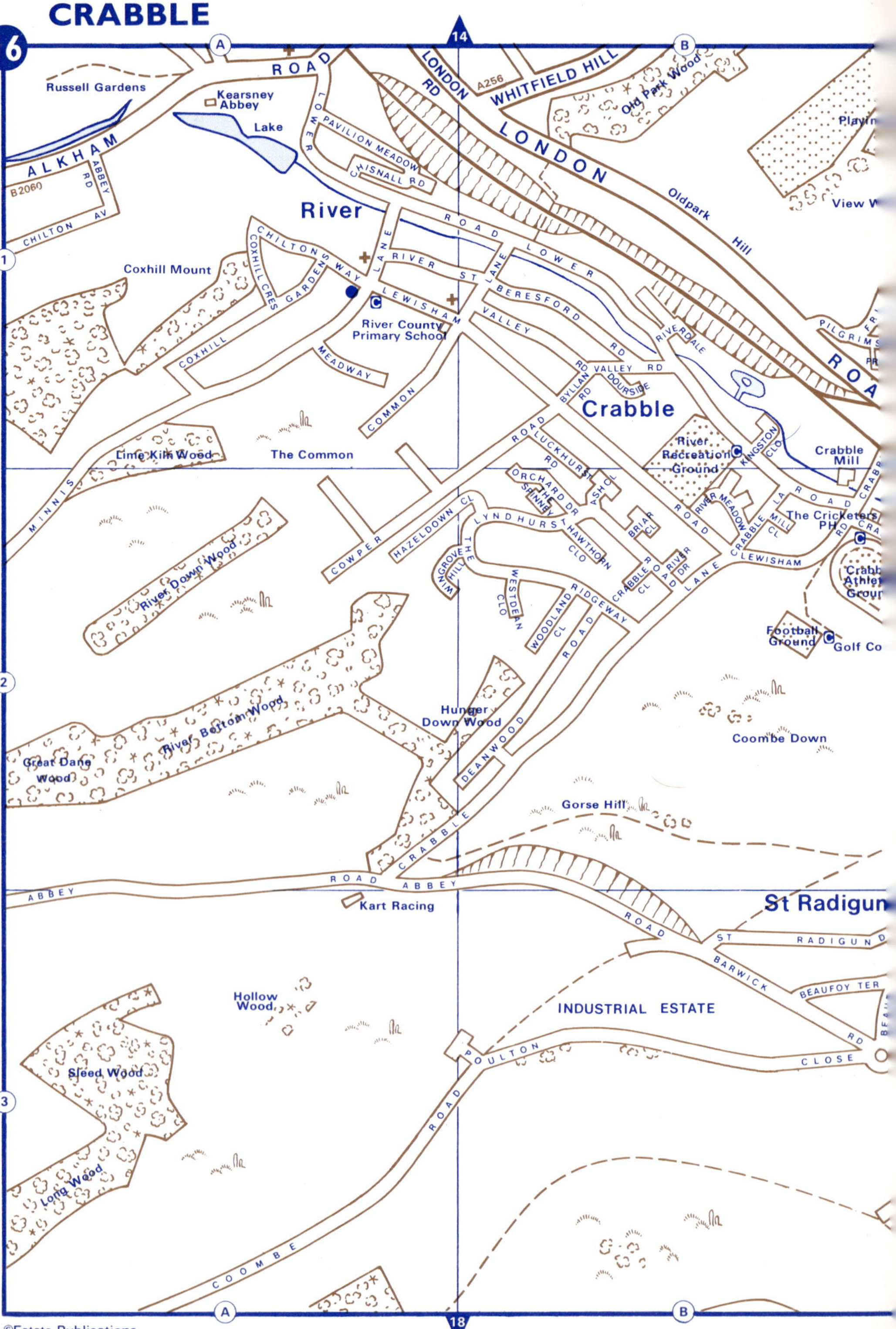
14
18
A
B
1
2
3
Russell Gardens
Kearsney Abbey
Lake
ALKHAM ROAD
ABBEY RD
B2060
CHILTON AV
LOWER ROAD
PAVILION MEADOW
CHISNALL RD
LONDON RD
A256
WHITFIELD HILL
LONDON ROAD
Old Park Wood
Oldpark Hill
Playin
View W
River
Coxhill Mount
CHILTON WAY
COXHILL CRES
CHILTON GARDENS
COXHILL
LANE
RIVER ST
LEWISHAM RD
River County Primary School
MEADWAY
COMMON LANE
BERESFORD RD
VALLEY RD
RIVERDALE
BYLLAN RD
DOURSIDE
Crabble
Lime Kiln Wood
The Common
ROAD
LUCKHURST RD
ORCHARD DR
THE SPINNEY
ASH CL
River Recreation Ground
KINGSTON CLO
Crabble Mill
The Cricketers PH
RIVER MEADOW
CRABBLE MILL CL
CRABBLE RD
MINNIS
HAZELDOWN CL
LYNDHURST
COWPER
HAWTHORN CLO
BRIAR CL
RIVER DR
LEWISHAM
WINGROVE
THE HILL
WESTDEAN CLO
WOODLAND CL
RIDGEWAY
CRABBLE CL
LANE
River Down Wood
Crabb Athle Groun
Football Ground
Golf Co
River Bottom Wood
Hunger Down Wood
DEANWOOD
Great Dane Wood
Coombe Down
Gorse Hill
CRABBLE
ABBEY ROAD
Kart Racing
St Radigun
ROAD
ST RADIGUND
BARWICK RD
BEAUFOY TER
Hollow Wood
INDUSTRIAL ESTATE
POULTON CLOSE
Sleed Wood
ROAD
Long Wood
COOMBE

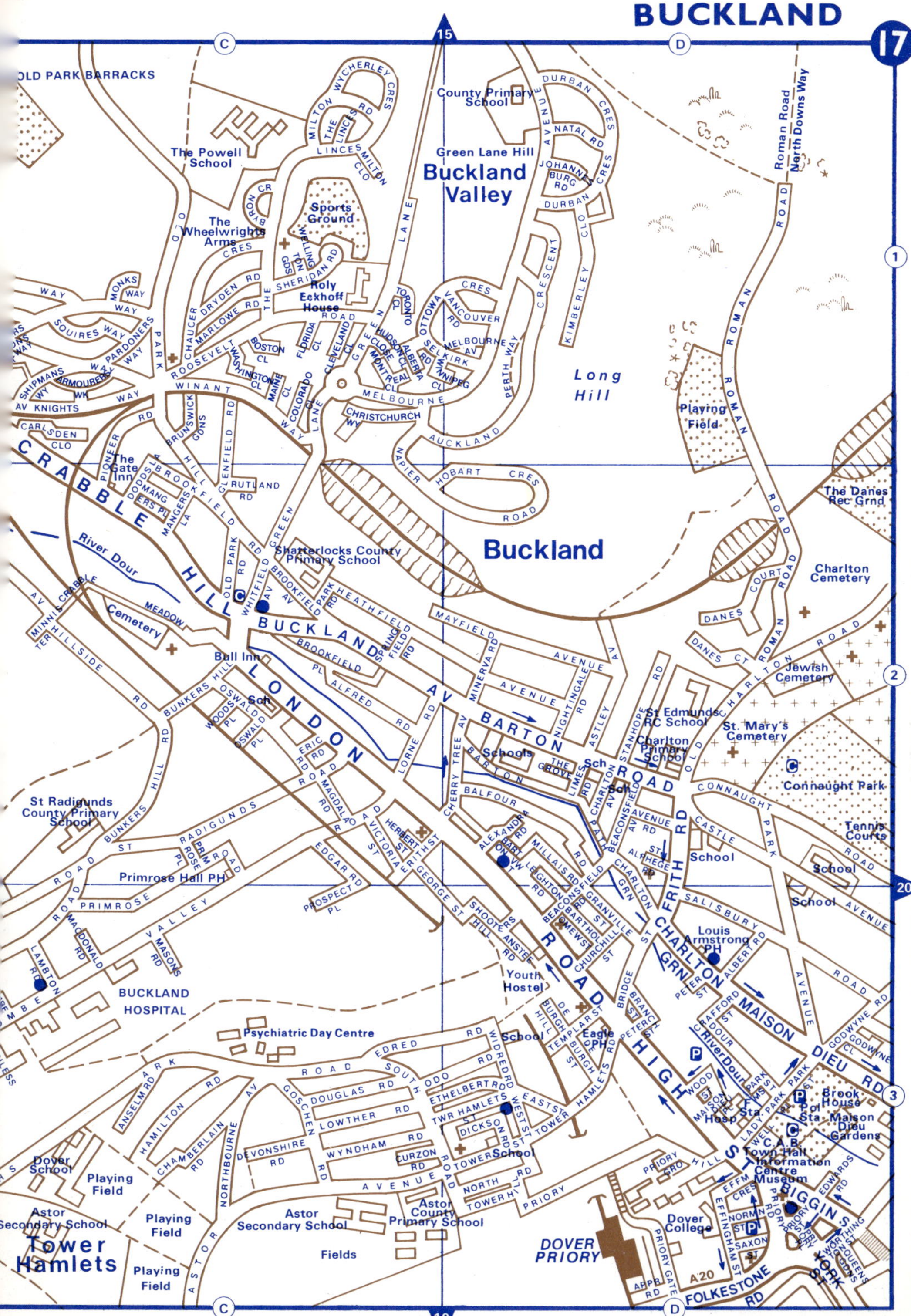

C
15
D
OLD PARK BARRACKS
The Powell School
County Primary School
Green Lane Hill
Buckland Valley
Sports Ground
The Wheelwrights Arms
Roly Eckhoff House
Long Hill
Playing Field
Roman Road
North Downs Way
The Danes Rec Grnd
Charlton Cemetery
Jewish Cemetery
Buckland
Shatterlocks County Primary School
The Gate Inn
River Dour
Cemetery
Bull Inn
Sch
CRABBLE HILL
BUCKLAND
LONDON ROAD
St Radigunds County Primary School
Primrose Hall PH
BUCKLAND HOSPITAL
Psychiatric Day Centre
Youth Hostel
Schools
St Edmunds RC School
Charlton Primary School
St. Mary's Cemetery
Connaught Park
Tennis Courts
School
Louis Armstrong PH
Eagle PH
Brook House
Pol Sta
Maison Dieu Gardens
C.A.B.
Town Hall
Information Centre
Museum
Dover College
DOVER PRIORY
Dover School
Playing Field
Astor Secondary School
Astor County Primary School
Fields
Tower Hamlets
A20
FOLKESTONE RD
BIGGIN ST
YORK ST
HIGH ST
MAISON DIEU RD
CHARLTON GRN
FRITH RD
BARTON RD
1
2
3
20
19

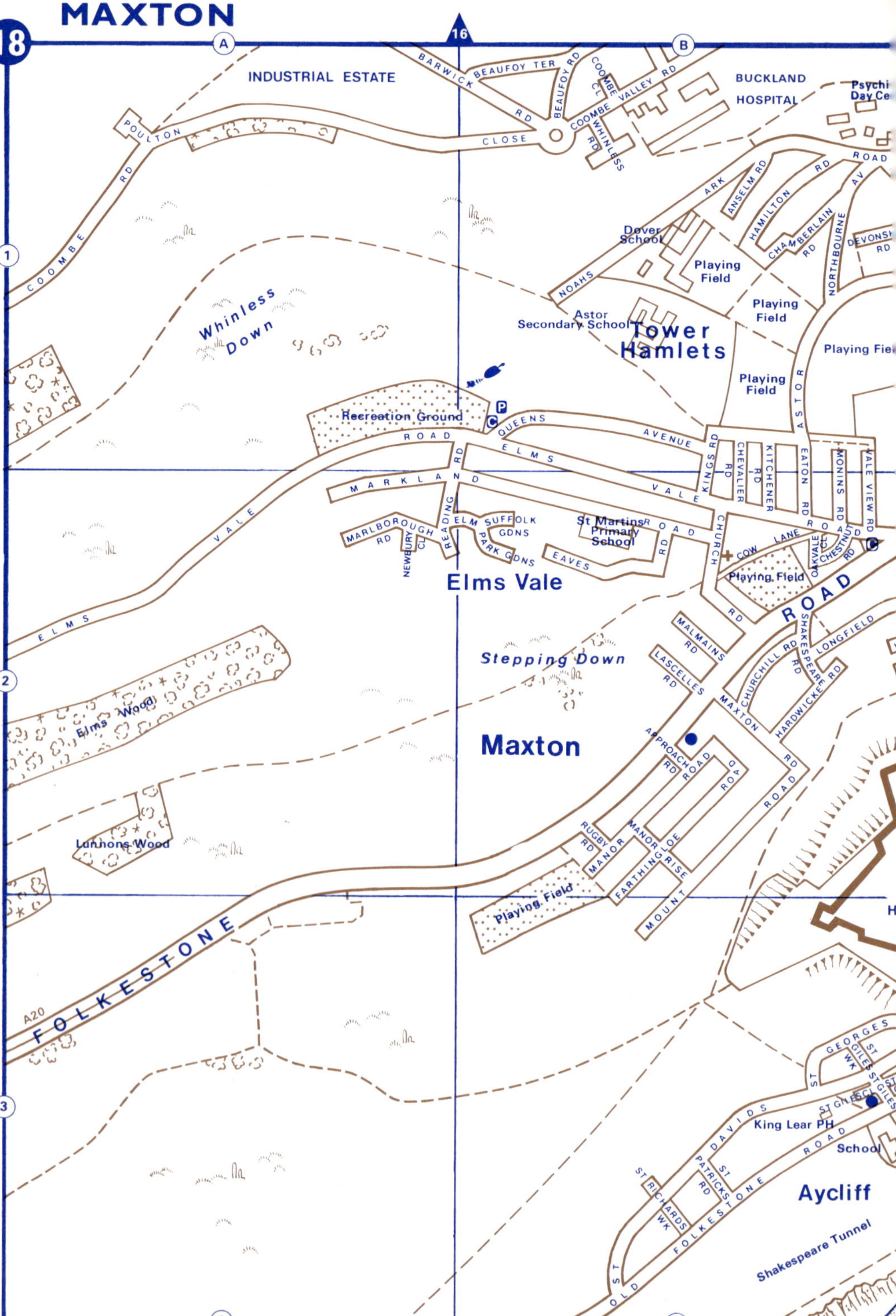
A
16
B
1
2
3
INDUSTRIAL ESTATE
BARWICK RD
BEAUFOY TER
BEAUFOY RD
COOMBE CL
COOMBE VALLEY RD
WHINLESS RD
BUCKLAND HOSPITAL
POULTON CLOSE
COOMBE RD
Whinless Down
ARK
NOAHS
ANSELM RD
HAMILTON RD
CHAMBERLAIN RD
NORTHBOURNE AV
DEVONSHIRE RD
ROAD
Dover School
Playing Field
Astor Secondary School
Tower Hamlets
Playing Field
Playing Field
ASTOR
Recreation Ground
QUEENS AVENUE
ROAD
ELMS
MARKLAND RD
KINGS RD
CHEVALIER RD
KITCHENER RD
EATON RD
MONINS RD
VALE VIEW RD
VALE
MARLBOROUGH RD
NEWBURY CL
READING RD
ELM PARK GDNS
SUFFOLK GDNS
St Martins Primary School
ROAD
EAVES RD
CHURCH RD
COW LANE
OAKVALE CL
CHESTNUT RD
Playing Field
Elms Vale
ELMS VALE
ROAD
MALMAINS RD
LASCELLES RD
CHURCHILL RD
SHAKESPEARE RD
LONGFIELD
HARDWICKE RD
Stepping Down
Elms Wood
Maxton
MAXTON RD
APPROACH RD
ROAD
ROAD
ROAD
Lunhons Wood
RUGBY RD
MANOR
MANOR RISE
FARTHINGLOE
MOUNT
Playing Field
A20
FOLKESTONE
ST GEORGES
GILES WK
ST GILES CL
ST GILES RD
ST DAVIDS
King Lear PH
ROAD
School
ST PATRICKS RD
ST RICHARDS WK
FOLKESTONE
Aycliff
OLD ST
Shakespeare Tunnel

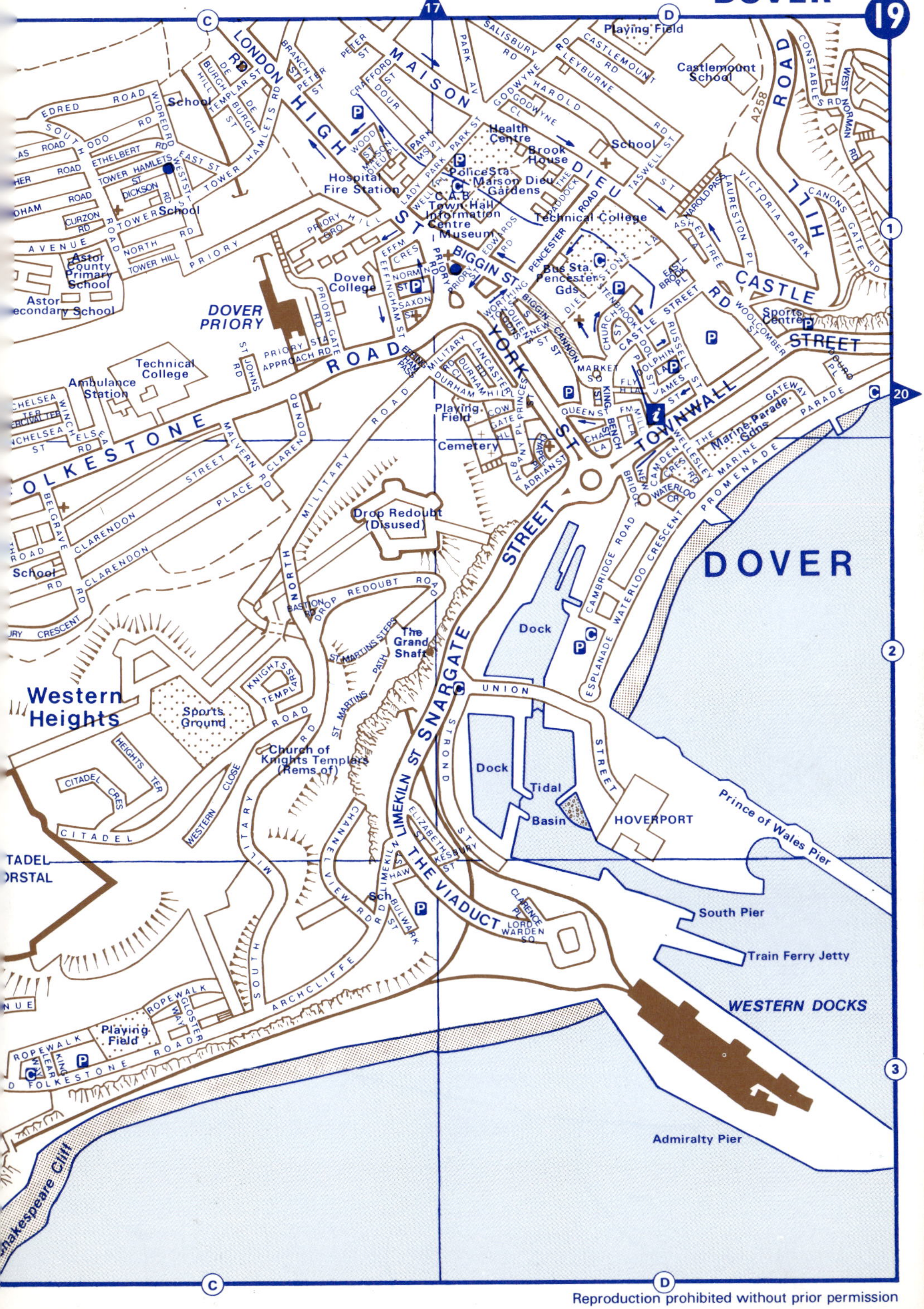
17
20
C
D
1
2
3
LONDON RD
HIGH ST
MAISON DIEU
BIGGIN ST
YORK ST
TOWNWALL
CASTLE ST
CASTLE HILL RD
STREET
FOLKESTONE ROAD
PRIORY
DOVER PRIORY
Dover College
Hospital
Fire Station
Police Sta.
Maison Dieu Gardens
C.A.B.
Town Hall
Information Centre
Museum
Health Centre
Brook House
School
Technical College
Bus Sta.
Pencester Gds
Castlemount School
Playing Field
Sports Centre
Marine Parade Gdns
MARINE PARADE
PROMENADE
Ambulance Station
Technical College
Astor County Primary School
Astor Secondary School
Cemetery
Drop Redoubt (Disused)
DROP REDOUBT ROAD
MILITARY ROAD
NORTH MILITARY RD
SNARGATE ST
UNION ST
STROND ST
LIMEKILN ST
THE VIADUCT
The Grand Shaft
Western Heights
Sports Ground
Church of Knights Templars (Rems of)
CITADEL
Dock
Tidal Basin
HOVERPORT
Prince of Wales Pier
South Pier
Train Ferry Jetty
WESTERN DOCKS
Admiralty Pier
DOVER
Shakespeare Cliff
ARCHCLIFFE
ROPEWALK
Playing Field
FOLKESTONE ROAD
CAMBRIDGE ROAD
WATERLOO CRESCENT
ESPLANADE
A258

DOVER

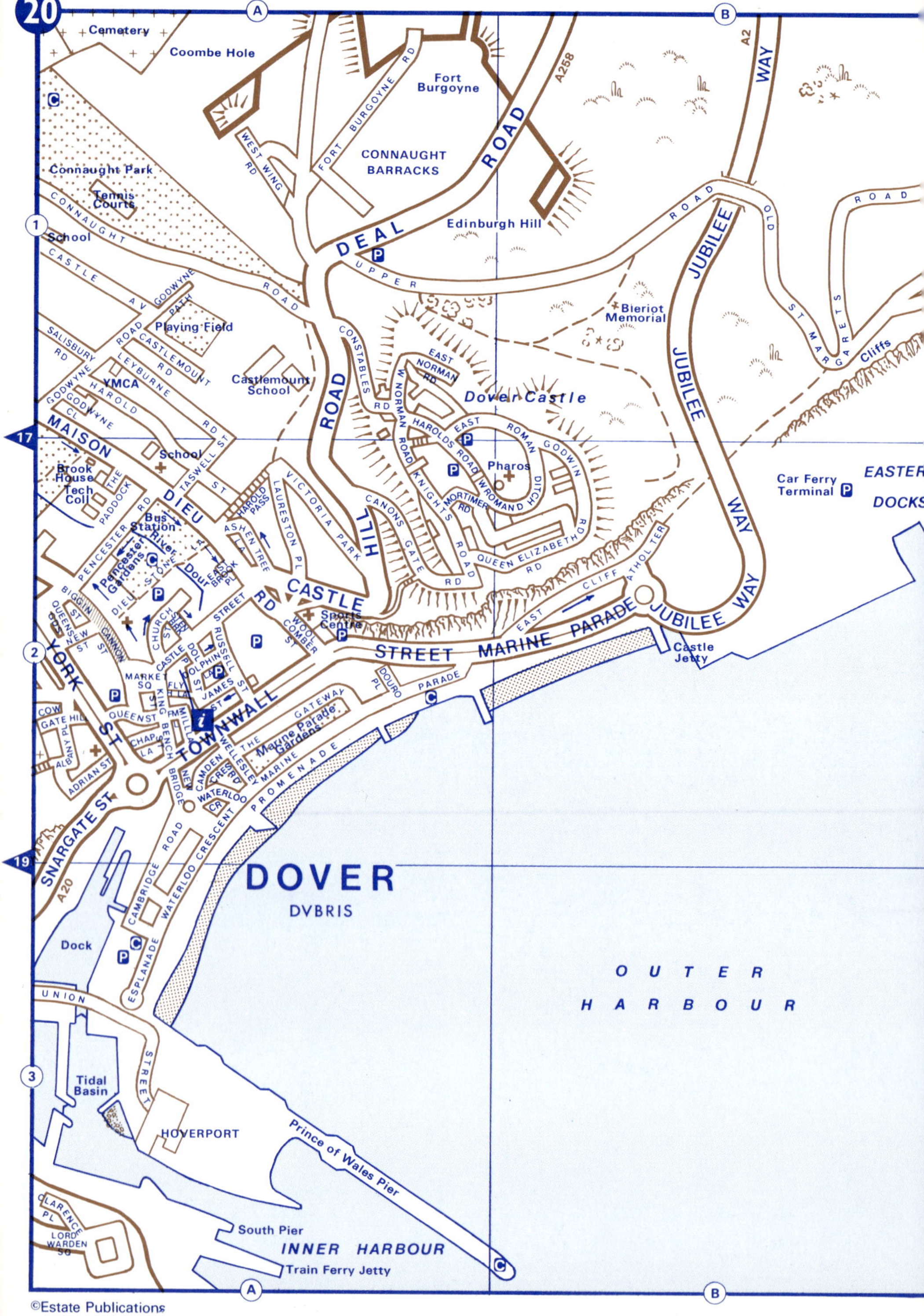
A
B
1
2
3
17
19
Cemetery
Coombe Hole
Fort Burgoyne
CONNAUGHT BARRACKS
FORT BURGOYNE RD
WEST WING RD
DEAL ROAD
A258
A2
WAY
Connaught Park
Tennis Courts
CONNAUGHT ROAD
School
CASTLE AV
GODWYNE PATH
Playing Field
Edinburgh Hill
UPPER ROAD
JUBILEE WAY
OLD ROAD
ST MARGARETS
Cliffs
Bieriot Memorial
SALISBURY RD
ROAD
CASTLEMOUNT RD
LEYBURNE RD
YMCA
HAROLD
GODWYNE CL
GODWYNE
Castlemount School
CONSTABLES RD
EAST NORMAN RD
NORMAN ROAD
Dover Castle
HAROLDS ROAD
EAST ROMAN
GODWIN
Pharos
ROMAN
DITCH
KNIGHTS ROAD
MORTIMER RD
QUEEN ELIZABETH RD
CANONS GATE RD
MAISON DIEU
Brook House
Tech Coll
THE PADDOCK
School
TASWELL ST
HAROLD PASS
VICTORIA PARK
LAURESTON PL
ASHEN TREE LA
CASTLE HILL
Car Ferry Terminal
EASTERN DOCKS
Bus Station
River
Dour
PENCESTER RD
Pencester Gardens
STONE LA
EAST BROOK PL
CASTLE RD
CASTLE STREET
Sports Centre
WOOLCOMBER ST
CLIFF
ATHOL TER
JUBILEE WAY
EAST
MARINE PARADE
Castle Jetty
BIGGIN ST
QUEENS GDNS
NEW ST
CANNON ST
DIEU
CHURCH ST
STREET
RUSSELL ST
YORK ST
MARKET SQ
DOLPHIN LA
DOLPHIN PL
JAMES ST
DOURO PL
PARADE
GATEWAY
Marine Parade Gardens
COW GATE HILL
ALBANY PL
QUEEN ST
KING ST
FLY
MILL LA
TOWNWALL
THE
WELLESLEY RD
CAMDEN CRES
NEW BRIDGE
BENCH ST
CHAPEL LA
ADRIAN ST
WATERLOO CR
MARINE
PROMENADE
SNARGATE ST
ROAD
WATERLOO CRESCENT
CAMBRIDGE RD
A20
DOVER
DVBRIS
Dock
ESPLANADE
OUTER HARBOUR
UNION STREET
Tidal Basin
HOVERPORT
Prince of Wales Pier
CLARENCE PL
LORD WARDEN SQ
South Pier
INNER HARBOUR
Train Ferry Jetty

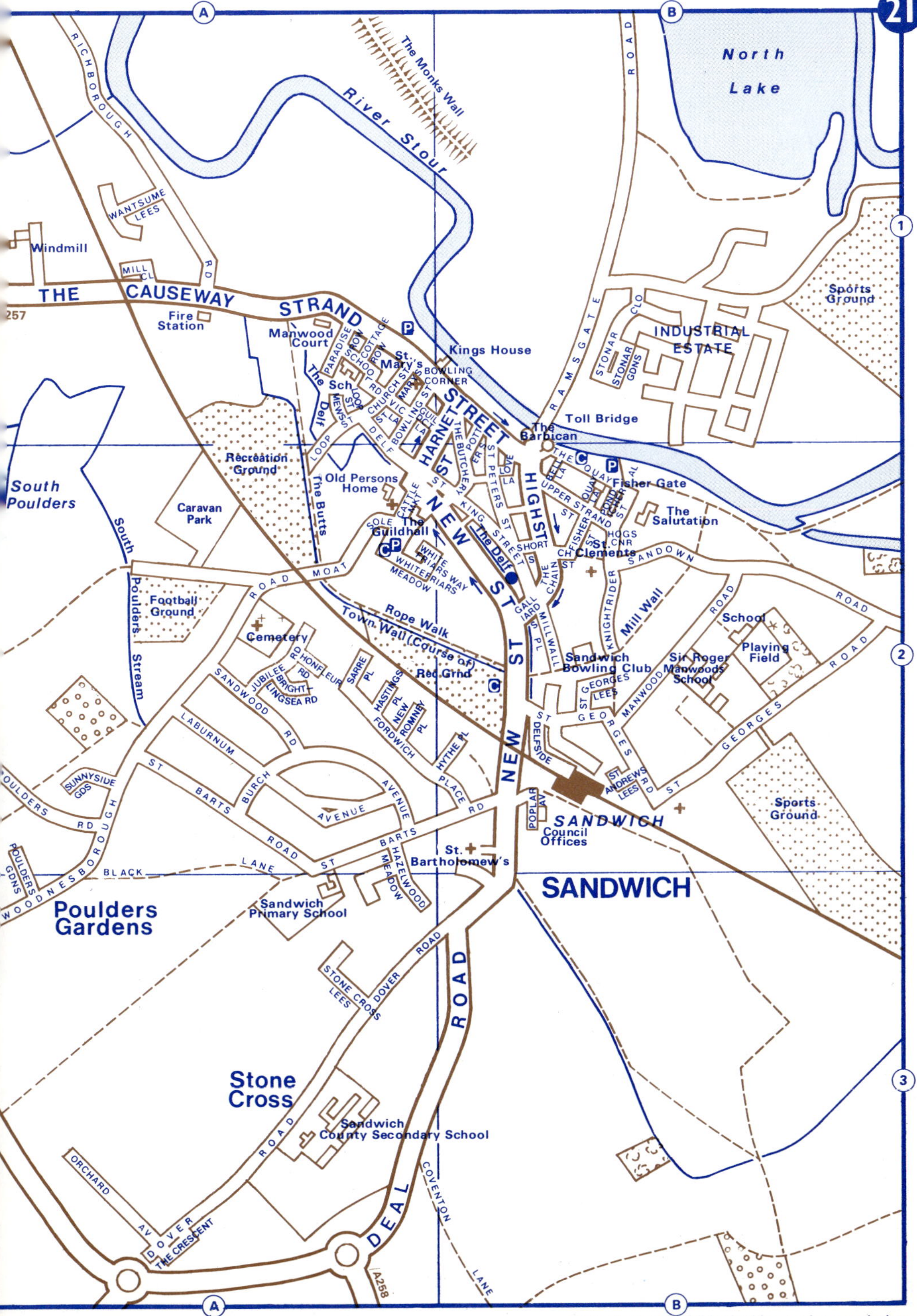
North Lake
River Stour
The Monks Wall
RICHBOROUGH RD
WANTSUME LEES
Windmill
MILL CL
THE CAUSEWAY
257
STRAND
Fire Station
Manwood Court
Kings House
St. Mary's
BOWLING CORNER
STREET
Toll Bridge
The Barbican
RAMSGATE ROAD
INDUSTRIAL ESTATE
STONAR CLO
STONAR GDNS
Sports Ground
Recreation Ground
The Delf
Old Persons Home
HARNET ST
THE BUTCHERY
POTTERS
ST PETERS ST
LOVE LA
HIGH ST
THE QUAY
Fisher Gate
The Salutation
UPPER STRAND ST
FISHER ST
St. Clements
HOGS CNR
SANDOWN ROAD
South Poulders
Caravan Park
The Butts
The Guildhall
SOLE
CATTLE MKT
KING STREET
SHORT ST
THE CHAIN
WHITE FRIARS WAY
WHITEFRIARS MEADOW
NEW ST
South Stream
Poulders Stream
Football Ground
MOAT ROAD
Rope Walk
Town Wall (Course of)
Cemetery
Red Grnd
MILLWALL PL
KNIGHTRIDER ST
Mill Wall
School
Playing Field
Sir Roger Manwoods School
Sandwich Bowling Club
ST GEORGES LEES
ST GEORGES RD
ST GEORGES ROAD
MANWOOD ROAD
JUBILEE RD
HONFLEUR RD
BRIGHT
LINGSEA RD
SARRE PL
HASTINGS PL
NEW ROMNEY PL
FORDWICH PL
HYTHE PL
SANDWOOD RD
LABURNUM
BURCH AVENUE
DELFSIDE
ST ANDREWS LEES
SUNNYSIDE GDS
POULDERS RD
POULDERS GDNS
ST BARTS ROAD
BARTS ST
PLACE RD
POPLAR AV
SANDWICH
Council Offices
St. Bartholomew's
HAZELWOOD MEADOW
BLACK LANE
WOODNESBOROUGH RD
Poulders Gardens
Sandwich Primary School
SANDWICH
STONE CROSS LEES
DOVER ROAD
DEAL ROAD
Stone Cross
Sandwich County Secondary School
ORCHARD AV
DOVER RD
THE CRESCENT
COVENTON LANE
A258
A
B
1
2
3

EASTRY

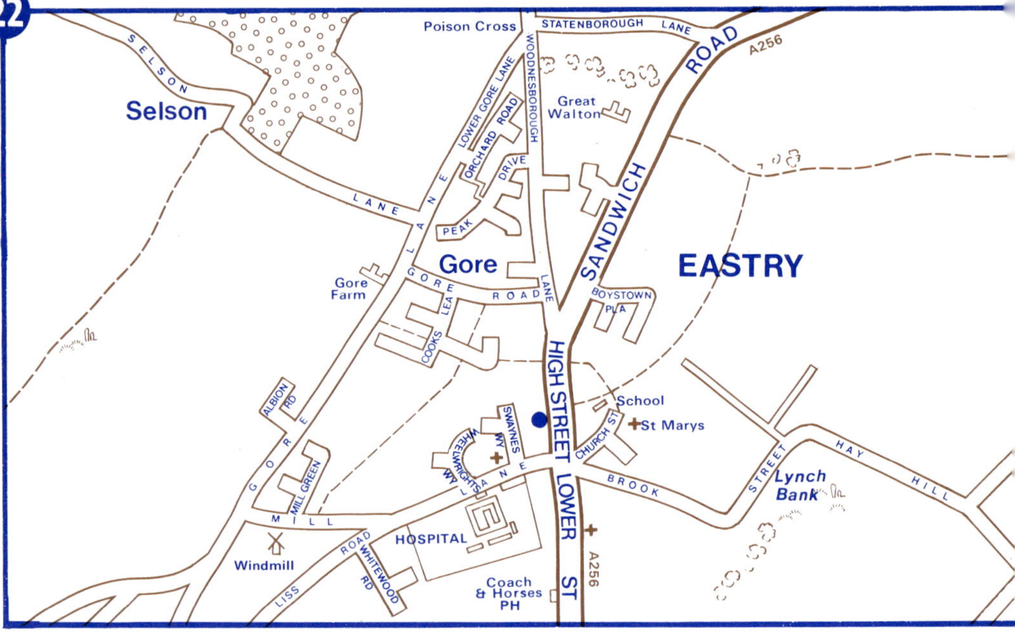

SHOLDEN

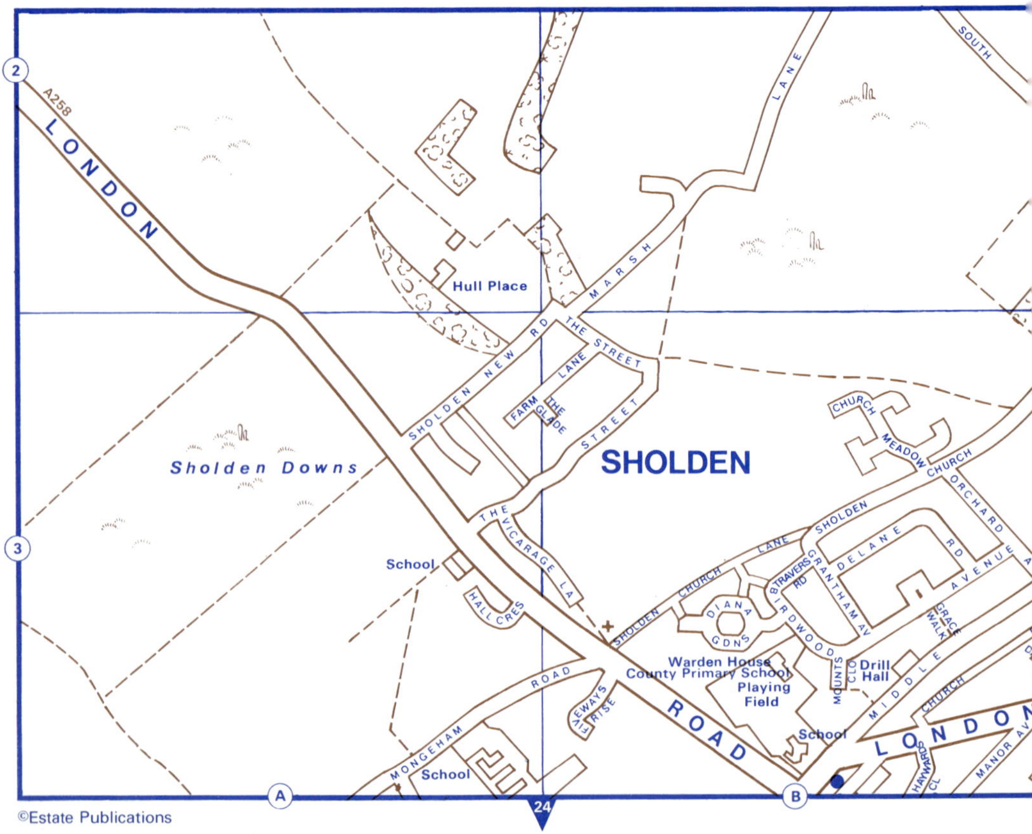

24

Royal Cinque Ports
Golf Club
Sandown Castle
(Site of)
REDHOUSE WALL
GOLF
CANUTE RD
Min. Golf Course
SANDOWN
ETHELBERT RD
GODWYN ROAD
SAXON PL
EDWARD RD
KING PL
VERNON
THE
HAROLD ROAD
COLLEGE
SANDOWN RD
GOLF ROAD
LINKS ROAD
BRIT ANNIA RD
ALBION RD
Coastguard Station
GOLF RD PL
ATHELSTAN PL
HORSA RD
THE FAIRWAY
SYDENHAM RD
HENGIST
WEST LEA
NORTH LEA
CANNON ST
ENFIELD
BRIDGE
DIBDEN
CAPSTAN ROW
North Deal County Primary School
ARK LA
PETER ST
ALFRED SQ
MARINA
THE DOWNS
North Deal Playing Field
WATER ST
GRIFFIN ST
PORTOBELLO CT
CLARENCE PL
NELSON
ROBERTS
SILVER
BEACH
DUKE ST
FARRIER ST
School
COPPIN ST
BREWER
UNION RD
ST PATRICKS RD
ST ANDREWS RD
ST DAVIDS RD
WESTERN RD
Maritime Museum
Town Hall
OAK ST
Royal Hotel
Bus Depot
MATTHEWS CL
ST GEORGES
CENTURY WK
STANHOPE RD
GEORGE ALLEY
KING ST
SOUTH STREET
BRIDGE SIDE
ANCHOR LA
PARK ST
Promenade Pier
SOUTHWALL RD
DEAL
School
BROAD ST
SUTHERLAND RD
THE TAR PATH
ALBERT RD
Fire Sta
QUEEN ST
ROAD
Municipal Offices
DEAL
VICTORIA PARADE
PR. OF WALES TER
GROVE
SOUTH ST
WELLINGTON RD
SONDES ROAD
STANLEY RD
CLANWILLIAM RD
RANELAGH ROAD
Queens Hotel
Police Station
BEECHWOOD AV
School
Middle Deal
COWPER RD
CHURCH
GRANGE RD
Bowls Grn
THE DRIVE
Tennis Courts
BLENHEIM
NORTH COTE RD
BEACONSFIELD RD
VICTORIA RD
HIGH ST
CLAREMONT RD
Youth Club
LISTER CLO
MILL
Victoria Park
Playground
HOPE ROAD
DEAL CASTLE ROAD
GREEN LA
LONDON
VICTORIA HOSPITAL
AVENUE
GILFORD RD
DOUGLAS TER
Deal Castle
PARK
GRANVILLE ST
GLADSTONE RD
THE STRAND
MARINE RD
ALLENBY AV
WILTON RD
LEAS RD
Victoria Park
RAVENSCOURT RD
A258
C
D
1
2
3
25

GT. MONGEHAM

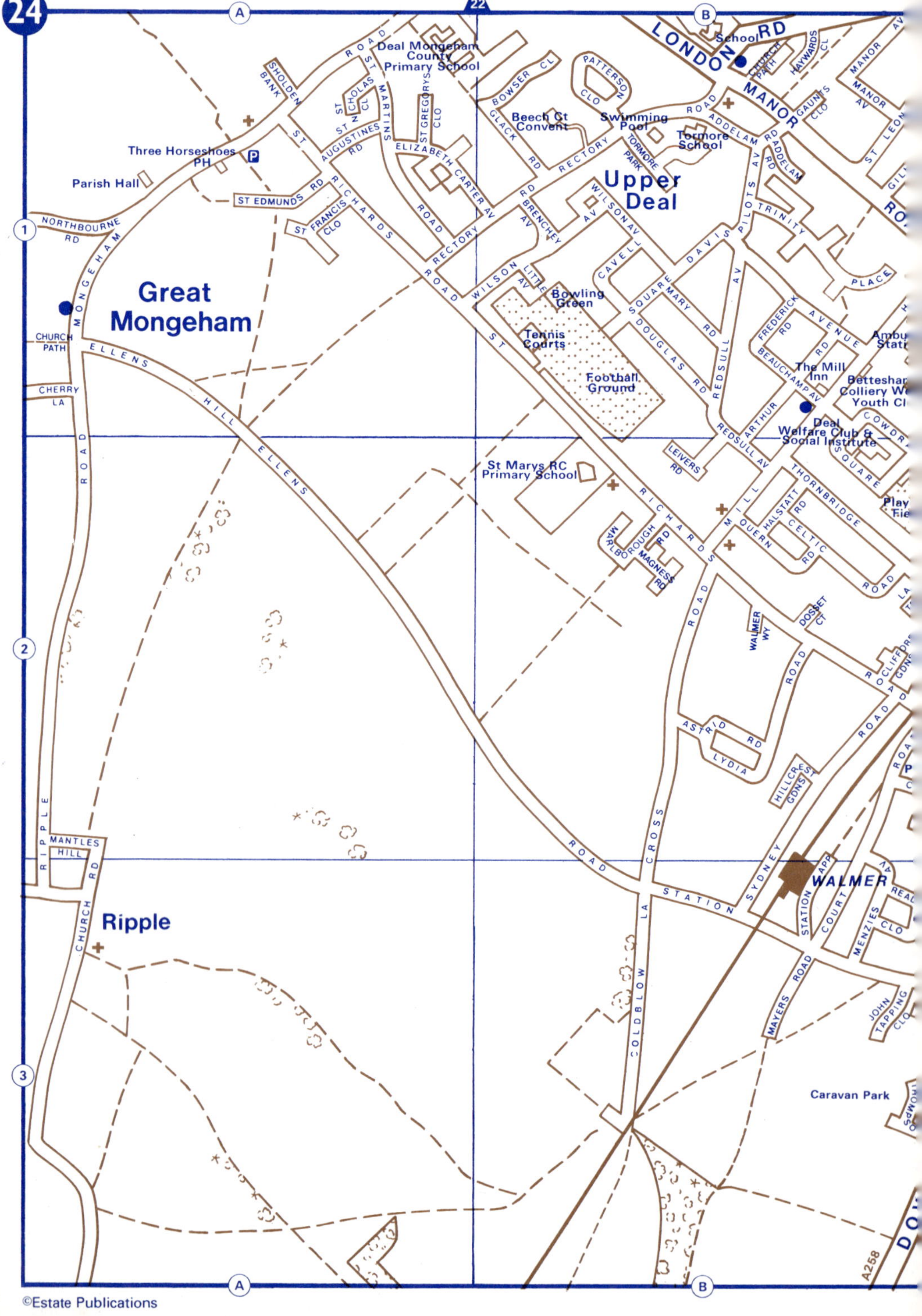
A
B
22
1
2
3
Great Mongeham
Upper Deal
Ripple
WALMER
Deal Mongeham County Primary School
Three Horseshoes PH
Parish Hall
Beech Ct Convent
Swimming Pool
Tormore School
School
Bowling Green
Tennis Courts
Football Ground
The Mill Inn
Betteshanger Colliery Welfare Youth Club
Deal Welfare Club & Social Institute
St Marys RC Primary School
Caravan Park
LONDON RD
MANOR RD
NORTHBOURNE RD
MONGEHAM ROAD
CHURCH PATH
CHERRY LA
ELLENS HILL
ELLENS ROAD
RIPPLE RD
MANTLES HILL
CHURCH RD
SHOLDEN BANK
ROAD
ST NICHOLAS CL
ST MARTINS
ST AUGUSTINES RD
ST GREGORYS CLO
ELIZABETH CARTER AV
ST EDMUNDS RD
ST FRANCIS CLO
ST RICHARDS ROAD
RECTORY RD
BOWSER CL
GLACK RD
PATTERSON CLO
TORMORE PARK
ADDELAM RD
BRENCHLEY AV
WILSON AV
LITTLE AV
CAVELL SQUARE
DAVIS AV
PILOTS AV
TRINITY PLACE
MARY RD
DOUGLAS RD
REDSULL AV
FREDERICK RD
BEAUCHAMP AV
AVENUE
ARTHUR RD
LEIVERS RD
COWDRAY SQUARE
THORNBRIDGE ROAD
HALSTATT RD
QUERN RD
CELTIC RD
MILL ROAD
MARLBOROUGH RD
MAGNESS RD
WALMER WY
DOSSET CT
CLIFFORD GDNS
ASTRID RD
LYDIA RD
HILLCREST GDNS
CROSS ROAD
SYDNEY RD
STATION ROAD
STATION APP
COURT RD
MENZIES CLO
MAYERS ROAD
COLDBLOW LA
JOHN TAPPING CLO
GAUNTS CLO
HAYWARDS CL
CHURCH PATH
MANOR AV
ST LEONARDS
A258

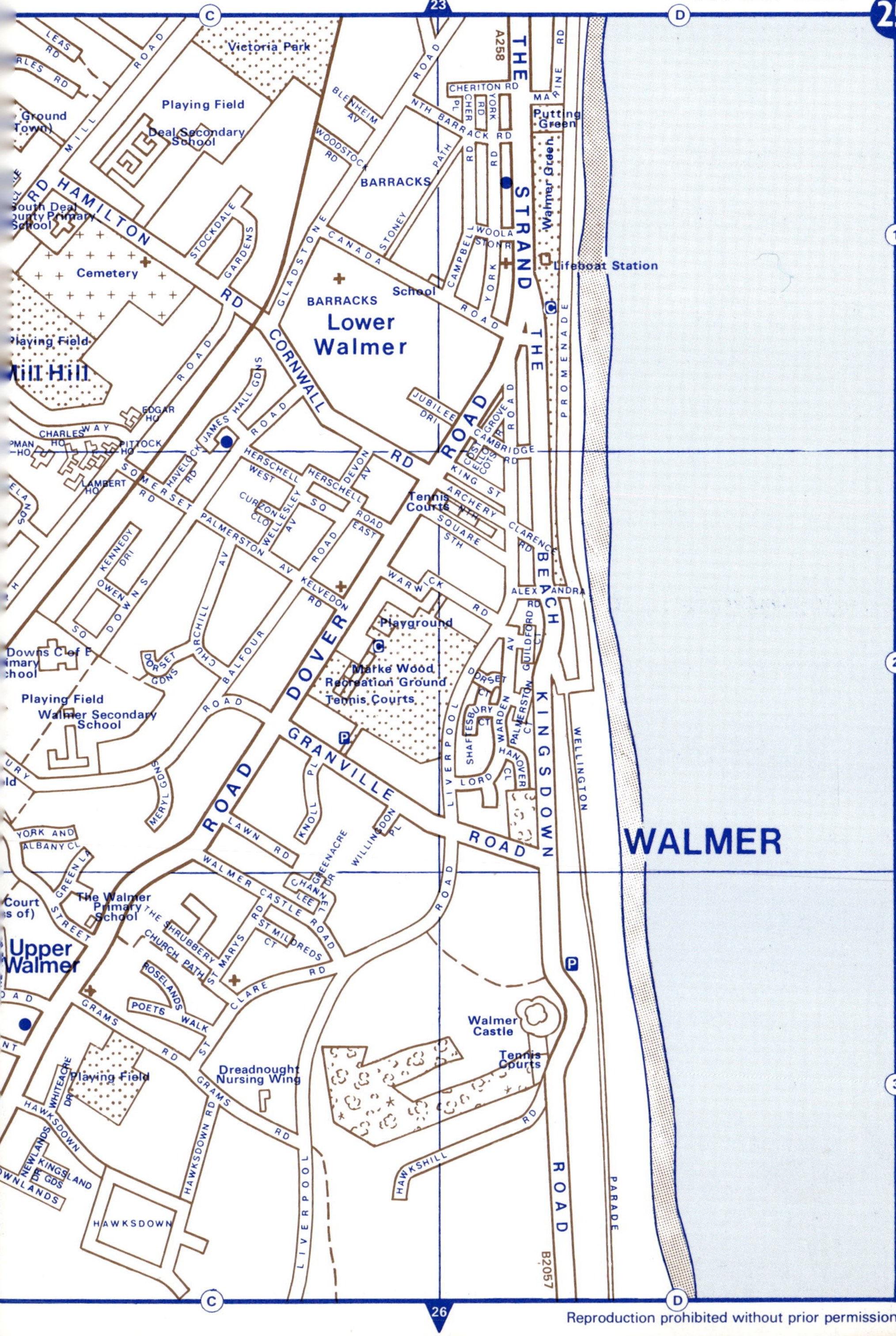
23
26
C
D
1
2
3
Victoria Park
Playing Field
Deal Secondary School
HAMILTON RD
South Deal County Primary School
Cemetery
Playing Field
Mill Hill
STOCKDALE GARDENS
MILL ROAD
LEAS RD
CHARLES RD
BLENHEIM AV
WOODSTOCK RD
BARRACKS
NTH BARRACK RD
PATH
STONEY
CANADA ROAD
GLADSTONE RD
CORNWALL RD
BARRACKS
Lower Walmer
School
CHERITON RD
CHERITON PL
YORK RD
A258
THE STRAND
MARINE RD
Putting Green
Walmer Green
Lifeboat Station
WOOLASTON RD
CAMPBELL RD
YORK RD
THE BEACH
PROMENADE
JUBILEE DRI
GROVE ROAD
CAMBRIDGE RD
KING ST
ARCHERY SQUARE NTH
ARCHERY SQUARE STH
Tennis Courts
CLARENCE RD
ALEXANDRA
DOVER ROAD
JAMES HALL GDNS
EDGAR HO
CHARLES WAY
PITTOCK HO
LAMBERT HO
HAVELOCK RD
SOMERSET RD
HERSCHELL RD WEST
HERSCHELL SQ
DEVON AV
HERSCHELL ROAD EAST
CURZON CLO
WELLESLEY AV
WELLESLEY ROAD
PALMERSTON AV
KENNEDY DRI
OWEN SQ
DOWNS
KELVEDON RD
WARWICK RD
Playground
Marke Wood Recreation Ground
Tennis Courts
CHURCHILL AV
BALFOUR ROAD
DORSET GDNS
Downs C of E Primary School
Playing Field
Walmer Secondary School
GRANVILLE ROAD
LIVERPOOL ROAD
DORSET CT
SHAFTESBURY CT
WARDEN CT
GUILDFORD AV
GUILDFORD CT
PALMERSTON CT
HANOVER CL
LORD
KINGSDOWN
WELLINGTON
MERYL GDNS
KNOLL PL
LAWN RD
GREENACRE DR
WILLINGDON PL
CHANNEL LEE
WALMER
YORK AND ALBANY CL
GREEN LA
STREET
The Walmer Primary School
Upper Walmer
THE SHRUBBERY
CHURCH PATH
ST MARYS RD
ST MILDREDS CT
WALMER CASTLE ROAD
ST CLARE RD
ROSELANDS
POETS WALK
GRAMS RD
Playing Field
WHITEACRE DR
Dreadnought Nursing Wing
GRAMS RD
HAWKSDOWN RD
HAWKSDOWN
NEWLANDS DR
KINGSLAND GDS
KINGSLAND
DOWNLANDS
Walmer Castle
Tennis Courts
HAWKSHILL RD
KINGSDOWN ROAD
B2057
PARADE
WALMER

KINGSDOWN

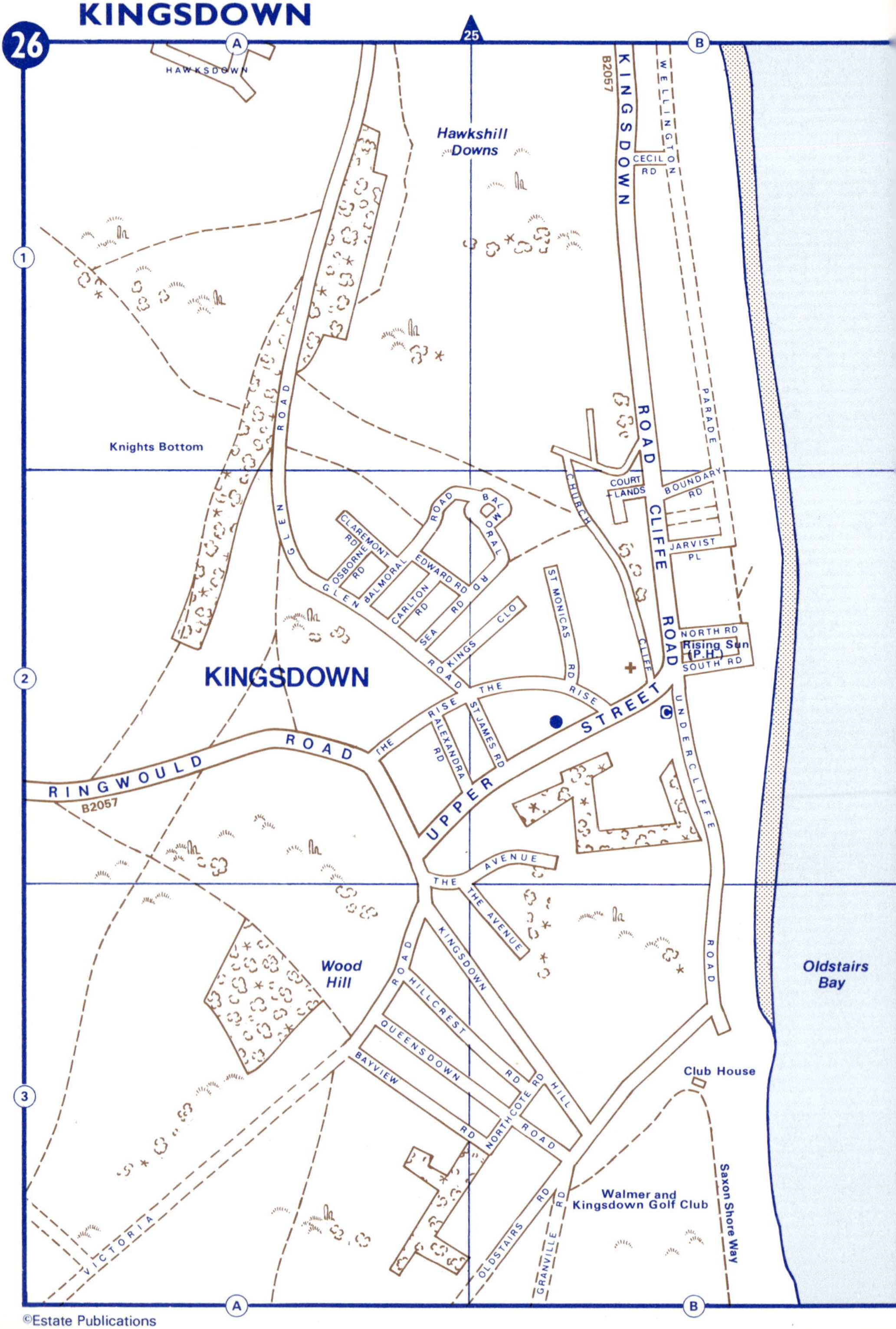
A
25
B
1
2
3
HAWKSDOWN
Hawkshill Downs
B2057
KINGSDOWN ROAD
WELLINGTON PARADE
CECIL RD
Knights Bottom
GLEN ROAD
CHURCH CLIFF
COURT LANDS
CLIFF ROAD
BOUNDARY RD
JARVIST PL
BALMORAL RD
CLAREMONT RD
OSBORNE RD
EDWARD RD
CARLTON RD
SEA RD
KINGS CLO
KINGS ROAD
ST MONICAS RD
NORTH RD
Rising Sun (P.H.)
SOUTH RD
KINGSDOWN
THE RISE
ALEXANDRA RD
ST JAMES RD
RINGWOULD ROAD
B2057
UPPER STREET
UNDERCLIFFE ROAD
THE AVENUE
Wood Hill
KINGSDOWN HILL
HILLCREST RD
QUEENSDOWN RD
BAYVIEW RD
NORTHCOTE ROAD
Club House
OLDSTAIRS RD
GRANVILLE RD
Walmer and Kingsdown Golf Club
Saxon Shore Way
Oldstairs Bay
VICTORIA

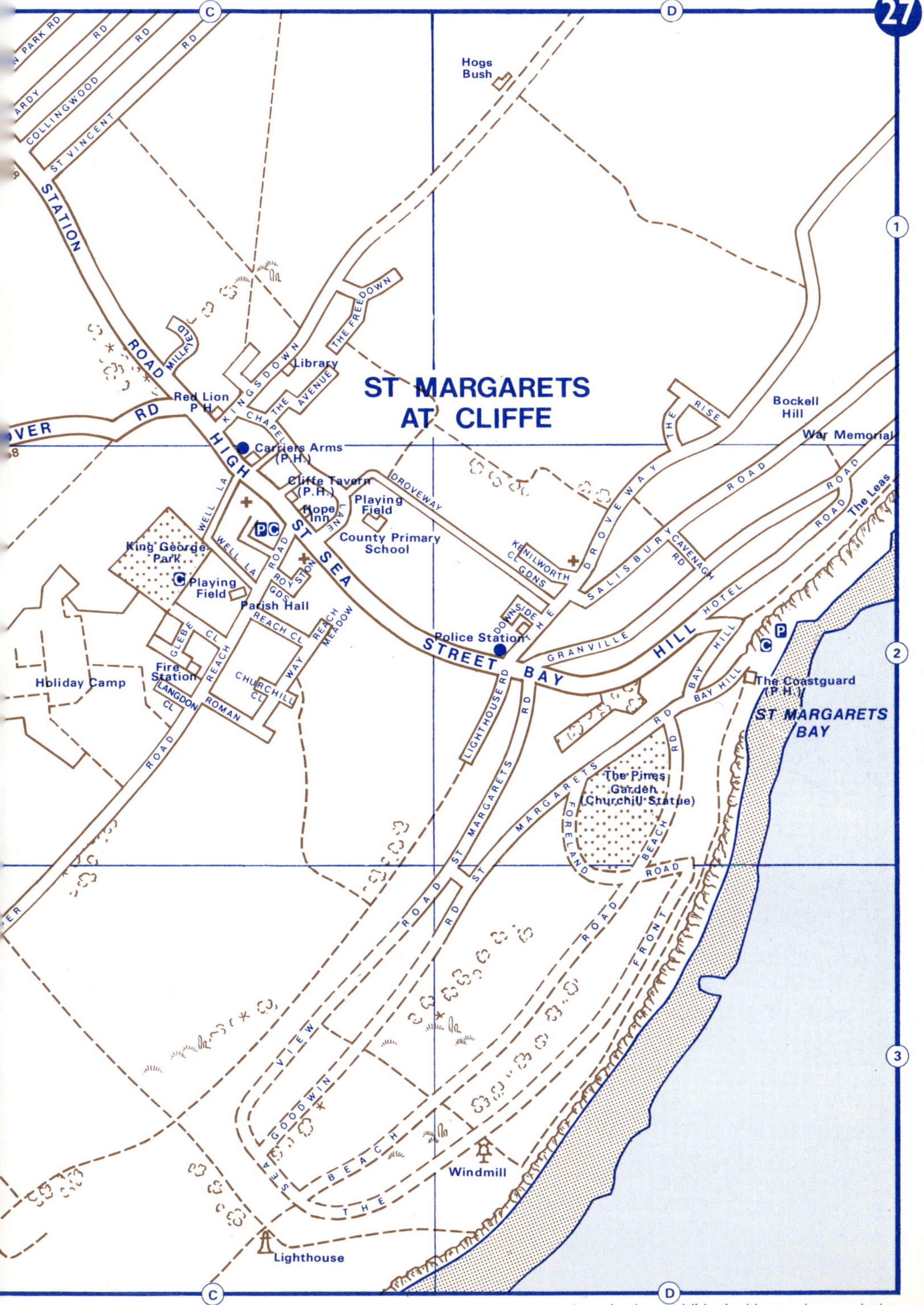
C
D
1
2
3
ST MARGARETS AT CLIFFE
Hogs Bush
STATION ROAD
ST VINCENT RD
COLLINGWOOD RD
MILLFIELD
DOVER RD
Red Lion P.H.
KINGSDOWN
Library
THE FREEDOWN
THE AVENUE
CHAPEL
HIGH ST
Carriers Arms (P.H.)
Cliffe Tavern (P.H.)
Hope Inn
LANE
Playing Field
County Primary School
DROVEWAY
WELL LA
King George Park
Playing Field
ROYSTON GDS
Parish Hall
REACH CL
REACH MEADOW
GLEBE CL
Fire Station
LANGDON CL
Holiday Camp
REACH ROAD
CHURCHILL CL
WAY
ROMAN
SEA STREET
Police Station
DOWNSIDE
THE
KENILWORTH GDNS CL
THE DROVEWAY
THE RISE
Bockell Hill
War Memorial
SALISBURY ROAD
CAVENAGH RD
ROAD
The Leas
GRANVILLE
HOTEL HILL
BAY HILL
BAY HILL
The Coastguard (P.H.)
ST MARGARETS BAY
LIGHTHOUSE RD
BAY
RD
ST MARGARETS RD
ST MARGARETS ROAD
ST MARGARETS RD
The Pines Garden (Churchill Statue)
FORELAND
BEACH ROAD
ROAD
FRONT
GOODWIN
VIEW
SEA
THE BEACH
Windmill
Lighthouse

CAPEL LE FERNE

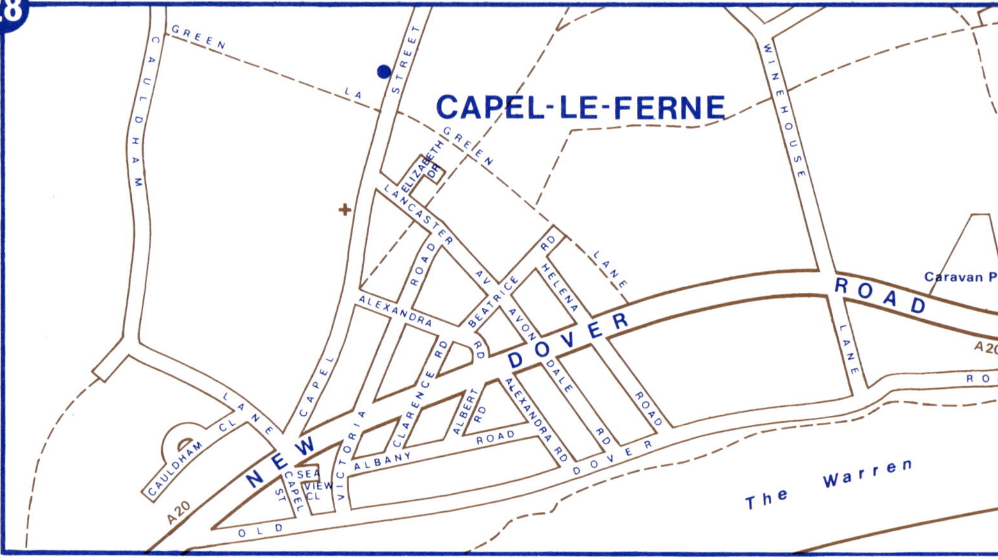

AYLESHAM

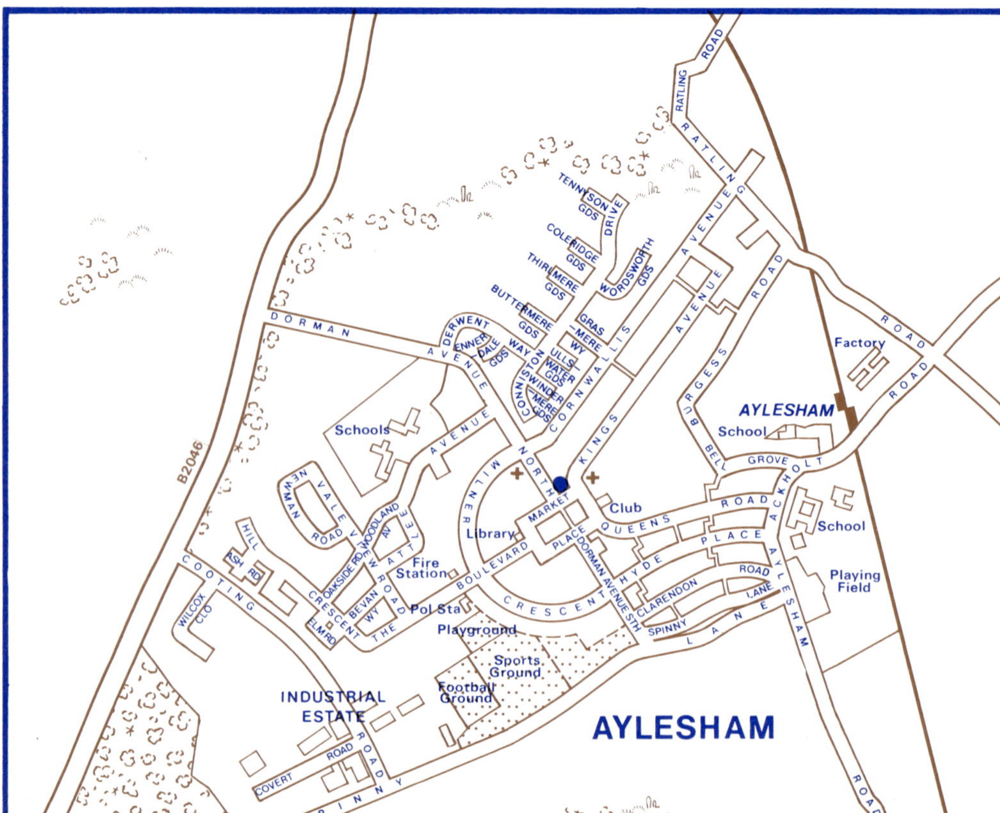

INDEX TO STREETS

DEAL

DOVER

FOLKESTONE & HYTHE

KINGSDOWN

ST. MARGARET'S AT CLIFFE

SANDWICH